TRISTRAM SHANDY

NOTES

including
- *The Life of Sterne*
- *Critical Introduction*
- *List of Characters*
- *Outline-Key to* Tristram Shandy
- *A Note on the Text*
- *Summaries and Commentaries*
- *Review Questions and Essay Topics*
- *Selected Bibliography*

by
Charles Parish, Ph.D.
Department of English
Southern Illinois University

INCORPORATED

LINCOLN, NEBRASKA 68501

Editor

Gary Carey, M.A.
University of Colorado

Consulting Editor

James L. Roberts, Ph.D.
Department of English
University of Nebraska

ISBN 0-8220-1311-8
© Copyright 1968
by
C. K. Hillegass
All Rights Reserved
Printed in U.S.A.

1994 Printing

Cliffs Notes, Inc.   Lincoln, Nebraska

CONTENTS

"Tristram Shandy" Notes

THE LIFE OF STERNE

Laurence Sterne was born in Ireland in 1713, and he died in London in 1768. He might have died much earlier because of his weak lungs, especially considering how much he laughed, but he managed to live long enough to give his countrymen and the world two great books, *Tristram Shandy* and *A Sentimental Journey*.

The influence of these two books went beyond the country and century in which they were written. French, German, Italian, and English sentimental journeys were a glut on the literary market, and Tristram-Shandeism not only engendered hundreds of silly imitations in Sterne's own time, but it also influenced great writers down to the present—Goethe, Mann, Gide, Joyce, to mention a few.

Sterne was an unimportant person who suddenly became important —for many people, notorious—in 1759. His background was undistinguished. The son of an army ensign, he grew up in army garrisons. There he learned about soldiers, and without that knowledge and experience, he could not have made Uncle Toby and Corporal Trim as convincing as they are.

With the help of relatives, he went to Cambridge. After graduating (1737), he entered the Church of England and, again with the help of relatives, became vicar of Sutton (and subsequently, of Stillington) in Yorkshire. It was a comfortable enough way to make a living, and it did not require great effort or special piety. Several years later, he married a woman with whom he never got along, Elizabeth Lumley, and they had a child whom he adored, Lydia. It is quite unlikely that he could have gotten along with any woman who didn't match him in imagination, ingenuity, and capriciousness; as it was, Mrs. Sterne went officially mad for a period of time and was probably unofficially mad for most of her life. Sterne and his wife agreed not to disagree, but his happiest moments were those when they lived apart.

During his time of country living—pre-*Tristram Shandy* days—he consoled himself with the pleasure available in York. It was not London, but neither was it the backwoods. In addition, he had a special group of friends, a men's club, called the "Demoniacks," chief among whom was John Hall-Stevenson, the proprietor of a crazy castle named "Crazy Castle." Most likely they gathered to get away from their wives, to drink and carouse, and to pretend to be rakes; without doubt, they read to each other bawdy passages from their favorite books. One of the important consequences of this Symposium was the irreverent attitude toward literature, the willingness to poke fun at "important" authors and important people, that permeates *Tristram Shandy*. Imagining an ideal, appreciative audience is important to an author; whimsy that is directed toward a group of friends who understand and laugh in response has a greater chance of success.

When the first two books of *Tristram Shandy* were published in 1759, most readers were delighted. Some of them ceased to laugh, however, when they discovered that the writer was a parson of the church. At any rate, Sterne became a celebrity overnight, and many famous people — literati and nobility — received him and applauded him; they called him "Tristram" or "Parson Yorick," identifying him completely with his book. Samuel Johnson thought him smutty and too peculiar in his writing, but when Oliver Goldsmith suggested that Sterne was dull, Johnson replied, "Why, no, Sir." Sterne reveled in his popularity and prosperity, and he commuted between York and London, reaping the fruits of fame.

The years between 1759 and 1768 were intensely busy ones for him. He wrote his five installments of *Tristram,* several volumes of *Sermons of Mr. Yorick,* and at the end of the period, *A Sentimental Journey.* He struggled very hard to enjoy his life, having adequate proofs that it was not to last for very long; he hoped to find in relationships with women some recompense for the emptiness of his marriage. No doubt he did, since whatever was ideal in those relationships came in large part from his imagination.

Looking for a climate that would deal more gently with his damaged lungs, he spent a good deal of time between 1762 and 1765 in France. His wife and daughter were happy there, and he finally settled them there permanently. His time in France furnished him with the material for Bk. 7 of *Tristram* as well as for the charming and successful *Sentimental Journey.*

This latter volume, a slim one, has won the hearts of readers and critics consistently during its 200 years of existence (February, 1768). The delicacy of the book pleases everyone, but there is still a lot of Sternean muscle rippling robustly under the skin. The complexity of life throbs beneath the surface of *Tristram Shandy; A Sentimental Journey* gives us Sterne's warm and gentle farewell to a life that gave him much satisfaction and delight. He died less than a month after it was published, at the pinnacle of his fame.

CRITICAL INTRODUCTION

In many ways and for various reasons *Tristram Shandy* is one of the great books of prose fiction. In its humor, universality, and insight into humanity it reminds one of Petronius, Rabelais, Cervantes, Swift, and Joyce. In its concern with motives and with the psychology of the individual, in the writer's approach to the problems of novel writing, it makes great sense to the twentieth-century reader.

Perhaps the key to the enjoyment of *Tristram Shandy* is Literalness. If we believe everything we are told in the book, understand it in the way we are told to understand it, we will not become angry and frustrated the way most readers have for the past 200 years. The secret is not to bring usual attitudes or traditional judgments to the book, but rather to surrender to the writer. As the author himself says,

> I would go fifty miles on foot, for I have not a horse worth riding on, to kiss the hand of that man whose generous heart will give up the reins of his imagination into his author's hands, — be pleased he knows not why, and cares not wherefore.

There is great good fun in *Tristram Shandy*, but it comes from being in harmony with the author rather than from being contrary and rebellious. Most eighteenth- and nineteenth-century readers loved the tender, sentimental passages in the book, but they disliked the fun. They lost their tempers at the many calculated twistings and turnings of the story, at the many jokes (bawdy and shaggy-dog types) — in short, they disliked the author because he didn't write the kind of book they wanted. Many twentieth-century readers have felt the same.

There are certain problems in reading this novel, but they present a kind of complexity that can be pleasurable for the modern reader. The problems are these: the identity of the author, the point of the story, and many, many digressions from the apparent story.

The Identity of the Author. — The full title of this book is *The Life and Opinions of Tristram Shandy, Gentleman.* In spite of this very explicit title, most people have taken for granted that it is really the story of Laurence Sterne, the author of the book. Sterne complained that the world considered him more Shandean than he actually was, and conversely the world has considered *Tristram Shandy* more Sternean than it actually is. In most people's minds, author and book have interpenetrated to such an extent that one is considered an extension of the other. Nothing but confusion is gained from this idea about the book: if we think that we're sometimes reading autobiography, sometimes fiction, and sometimes a blend of the two, we cannot help but be uncertain and nervous about it.

The fullest and deepest meaning is gotten from the book only by assuming that Sterne created a fictional character named Tristram Shandy and that he made him a writer. He gave him a mind that knows of all the happenings in the book, and this mind is independent of the artist Sterne's mind. It is an artistic mind, somewhat like Sterne's, and it is a lucid and consistent one in spite of all the inconsistencies it shows. For the purposes of the reader, it is the mind of an individual named Tristram Shandy, not Laurence Sterne.

The thoughts and the opinions of Tristram Shandy, however much they may coincide with what we know of Laurence Sterne, belong primarily to the man who is the legitimate offspring of Mr. and Mrs. Walter Shandy and the nephew of Captain Toby Shandy. One could even say that Sterne created no other characters. Tristram, once his mind has been set in motion, creates the rest of the individuals who people his world, meaning that all of them come through to the reader through the unfolding of Tristram's consciousness. This creation by Tristram is one of the most important of the dynamic processes of the novel. Sterne writes about a man who is writing a book, and this man presents for the reader's inspection the people who had significance in his life; all of their stories are told to us directly or indirectly by this man. His life is tied up with theirs before he is born because he is presented to us as remembering this relationship. Thus, the first point to be taken literally in the title is that the author *within* the *Life and Opinions of Tristram Shandy, Gentleman* is Tristram Shandy. Whenever the term "author" is used hereafter, it will refer to Tristram and not to Laurence Sterne.

The Point of the Story. — About 10 years before the publication of *Tristram Shandy* (1759), Henry Fielding published his *History of Tom Jones, a Foundling* (1749). *Tom Jones* has always been the archetype of the "well-made novel," and for many readers and critics *Tristram Shandy* suffers by comparison with it. *Tom Jones* presents the "life and adventures" of its hero; everything happens in an orderly, progressive way. The hero appears as an infant in the third chapter, and the major part of the book deals with his adventures as a young man. But there is no such orderliness in *Tristram Shandy:* Tristram is born a third of the way through the book, and the last 45 chapters of the book (many of them short) deal with the events that took place five years before his birth. The stories of Mr. and Mrs. Shandy, of Uncle Toby and Corporal Trim, of Uncle Toby and the Widow Wadman, *and* the story of Tristram's childhood and young manhood itself, are all picked up, dropped, and picked up again and again. The author unhesitatingly tells the end of a story first, then the beginning, and then the middle; sometimes he tells the beginning and then drops it for a hundred pages. He manipulates the years and the events; he places, displaces, and replaces the people of his family (including himself) as he likes, taking them from the context of their actions and putting them back according to the way they figure in his reflections about them. Their stories give way for his opinions—the opinions of an author at work—and they are picked up according to his will and inserted into the pattern of his history as illustrations of his opinions. Everything, individuals and events, moves in direct response to the controlling consciousness of the author. He makes them move or he makes them stop in their tracks in mid-sentence; and when he thinks that it is time to go back to them, they start moving and they finish their sentence. The affairs of the lovable Shandy family and the goings-on at Shandy Hall are given to us piecemeal and topsy-turvy: now we see them, now we don't; we see them here, and suddenly we see them there.

But one person we always see and hear, no matter what happens to the Shandy family story, is Tristram, whose "life and opinions" continue unbroken. Whether or not anyone else is present, he is in *every* scene by means of his "my uncle Toby," "my father," "my mother." His presence is not merely a storyteller's point of view; writing of the components of his life at a distance as a mature man—and as a writer— he has the advantages of a mature man's outlook. Only he is alive at the time of writing; all the others have been long dead. The fact that he is able to conjure them up in all their vividness and move them backward and forward in "time" without impairing that vividness, demonstrates and proves the reality and depth of the character that Sterne created for him: he belongs to the Shandy family and he is also a clever writer. The Shandy ménages are important, but they are not more important than the thoughts they give rise to in the mind of this clever writer. And when these thoughts provoke a stream of thought which does not concern any Shandy other than Tristram the writer, goodbye to the

Shandys for a while. And the Shandys whom the writer bids goodbye to every so often include even *little* Tristram himself; the writer is willing to tell (with a calculated attempt to frustrate the reader) about his own conception, his birth, his childhood accidents, his first breeches, and a couple of trips to the Continent, but nothing else. It is *big* Tristram he is concerned with, and the opinions (i.e., ideas, fancies, prejudices, caprices) of this Tristram. He himself is the subject of his book, and his inner life and his opinions are the material that interests him most. So, the next point to be taken literally in the title is that the book is about the life and *opinions* of Tristram Shandy—just as it says. The title is a clue to Sterne's intentions. Tristram views his life through the medium of his opinions, and his opinions control the presentation of his reminiscences.

The Digressions.—The solution to the problem of the digressions follows from the above discussion of the problems of the identity of the author and the point of the story. Writing about his own life and his opinions, the author, Tristram, frees himself from the standard "life and adventures" approach. He is introspective about himself and his background and equally about the techniques of the book he is writing. He is the narrator of the "story," but he is also the conscious artist who is concerned with his ideas, with the ordering and significance of those ideas, and with the impact of those ideas both upon himself as artist and upon his "public." The digressions of *Tristram Shandy* are of two distinct types: the first take the reader from the immediate part of the story to antecedent or subsequent events that supposedly clarify or amplify the story; the second take the reader from the immediate story to the private views of the author, either on that story or on completely diverse subjects. But all of these digressions finally have unity in the creative consciousness of Tristram. No matter how digressive he may get, his constant effort—he tells us regularly—is aimed at the harmonizing of these digressions with the "main work"; and no matter how vague the connection is between "digression" and "story," he always finally brings the two together. In the meantime, how do you organize opinions? Unlike straight-line adventures, they resist coming to attention and forming orderly ranks. Further, how many opinions can fit into the book? As someone once said, "...the fragments of the narrative have the appearance of interruptions to digressions!" But this is Tristram's book, and that's the form he gave to it. We finally understand all about Tristram Shandy not only or primarily from the events of his life—his "story"—but from the book whose very structure reflects his mind and his character. Tristram says near the end of the book, "—All I wish is, that it may be a lesson to the world, *'to let people tell their stories in their own way.'*" The best thing of all, in reading his book, is to take his advice.

LIST OF CHARACTERS

The Shandy Household

Walter Shandy, father of Tristram. A man who loves hypotheses, theories, and erudition, and hates interruptions. He is an easily disappointed man.

Mrs. Shandy (Elizabeth), mother of Tristram. A singularly down-to-earth woman whose outstanding traits — if she has any — are her lack of imagination and her inability to ask an interesting question.

Captain Toby Shandy (retired), uncle of Tristram and brother of Walter. His main interest in life is fortifications and military history, and his character is one of gentleness and amiability.

Corporal Trim (James Butler), loyal servant and former companion-at-arms of Toby Shandy. An eloquent orator who shares his master's enthusiasm for past battles.

Susannah, the Shandy maidservant. A young woman who bustles about. She is the unwitting tool of various small disasters that strike the Shandy household.

Obadiah, the manservant. Another bustler, distinguished by frequent maladroitness and poor sense of timing.

The Scullion. A fat, simple kitchen servant.

Bobby Shandy, the older son of the Shandy family. Although he never appears in the book, his death is discussed in Bk. 4, Chap. 31.

Tristram Shandy No. 1. The "hero," who is born in Bk. 3, Chap. 23. Victim of small misfortunes that seem great ones to his father. We see him rarely; all there is to him is the series of Accidents, the question of whether his parents should put him into trousers, and the mention of a trip he took to France with his father and his Uncle Toby.

Friends, Neighbors, and Obstetricians

Parson Yorick, the village parson. Friend and level-headed adviser of the Shandy family, his iconoclastic wit makes many enemies.

Widow Wadman. A woman who has cold feet in bed. Disappointed in her first husband, she hopes to find a better one in Captain Toby Shandy.

Bridget, her maidservant. Sometime paramour of Corporal Trim.

Eugenius, a man of the world. Friend of Parson Yorick, he tries unsuccessfully to teach him caution and prudence.

Dr. Slop, the man-midwife. A very short, very fat obstetrician who attaches great importance to obstetrical instruments.

The Midwife. An old woman who assists at the delivery of Tristram.

The Curate (named "Tristram"). An officious person who baptizes Tristram.

Others

Aunt Dinah. The Shandy family scandal.

Lieutenant Le Fever. An unfortunate soldier, sustained in his last moments of life by Mr. Toby Shandy.

Billy Le Fever. Son of the above and recipient of the generous bounty of Mr. Toby Shandy.

Kysarcius

Phutatorius

> Learned men and acquaintances of Parson Yorick.

Didius

Gastripheres

AND

Tristram Shandy No. 2, the Author of *The Life and Opinions of Tristram Shandy, Gentleman.* Laurence Sterne's chief character, he tells the story of the people listed above, he makes judgments about the events of their lives, and he gives us the step-by-step details of the problems and difficulties involved in writing this sort of book.

Jenny. A casually mentioned young lady friend of the author.

OUTLINE-KEY TO *TRISTRAM SHANDY**

BOOK 1

(1) The author reflects upon the sad circumstances of his conception. (2) The author bemoans the vitiated homunculus and animal spirits. (3) How the preceding has been told to the author by his Uncle Toby. (4) Formal statement of the above for the benefit of readers who "find themselves ill at ease, unless they are let into the whole secret from first to last." (5) The author says he was born November 5, 1718. (6) The author prepares the reader for his donning the "fools-cap." (7) The installation of the midwife by the parson's wife. (8) A statement on hobby-horses, plus a Dedication. (9) Remarks on the preceding Dedication, its virginity and its value. (10) Fruitless return to the midwife; the story of Yorick's fine horses. (11) Yorick the jester and Yorick the parson. (12) Yorick's humor, its consequences, and his sad death (1748). (13) Second fruitless return to the midwife. (14) Difficulties of an author; despair at ever catching up: "I have been at it these six weeks...and am not yet born." (15) Mrs. Shandy's marriage settlement; her right to lie-in in London. (16) False-alarm and the return from London. (17) Consolation for Walter Shandy: Lying-in in the country. (18) Anticipations of Walter Shandy on his wife's lying-in in the country; his measures against careless delivery. (19) Walter Shandy on names good and evil; his unconquerable aversion for "Tristram." (20) The author on careless readers; "Les Docteurs de Sorbonne" on baptism. (21) First chapter on Tristram's birth; Uncle Toby knocks out his ashes, and says "I think——"; Uncle Toby's modesty concerning Aunt Dinah. (22) The author's statement on his work: "In a word, my work is digressive, and it is progressive too, —— and at the same time." (23) Reasons for drawing Uncle Toby's character from his hobby-horse. (24) The fact that Uncle Toby had a strange hobby-horse. (25) Uncle Toby's wound; the ease gained through telling about it. The author says that the reader cannot guess what he is about to say.

---

*From "A Table of Contents for *Tristram Shandy*" by Charles Parish, *College English,* XXII (December, 1960), 143-50. Reprinted by permission of the National Council of Teachers of English.

BOOK 2

(1) King William's Wars; Uncle Toby's idea of a map of Namur. (2) The author answers his critics; he says that his book, like Locke's is a "history-book...of what passes in a man's mind." (3) Uncle Toby's map; the broadening of his knowledge of fortifications. (4) The author explains why he ended the previous chapter at "the last spirited apostrophe"; how Uncle Toby mightily desires his health. (5) Trim incites Uncle Toby to go down to the country to build fortifications. (6) The end of Uncle Toby's sentence, "I think——" which began in Bk. 1, Chap. 21; a talk on modesty as a reason for Mrs. Shandy's preferring the midwife to Dr. Slop. (7) Modesty, cont'd; the right and wrong ends of a woman; Uncle Toby mentions his unfortunate experience with the Widow Wadman. (8) Concerning time ("an hour and a half's tolerable good reading"), and the hypercritic's pendulum. (9) Obadiah's collision with Dr. Slop. (10) Enter Dr. Slop; on Uncle Toby's train of thought (connecting Stevinus with the ring of the bell). (11) "Writing...is but a different name for conversation"; Dr. Slop has forgotten his bag. (12) Why Stevinus came into Uncle Toby's mind; patience and placidity of Uncle Toby shown by the episode of the fly; Walter repents his baiting of Uncle Toby and is forgiven. (13) " 'Tis not worth talking of." (14) Stevinus, cont'd. (15) The discovery of the Sermon upon Conscience. (16) How *Conscience* is upon neither side — neither Catholic nor Protestant. (17) Trim's stance and posture; the Sermon, with many interruptions; Trim's brother, Tom. (18) Obadiah's entrance with the bag; Uncle Toby's "I wish...you had seen what prodigious armies we had in *Flanders.*" (19) "I have dropp'd the curtain over this scene for a minute." Mr. Shandy's nicety in reasoning; the center of the brain is the medulla oblongata — proved at length.

BOOK 3

(1) Uncle Toby's wish, cont'd; Dr. Slop's "confusion." (2) Walter's challenging of the wish, and the reaching for a handkerchief. (3) Reaching for the handkerchief, cont'd. (4) The author on the relation of body and mind. (5) Reaching for the handkerchief, cont'd. (6) Walter's challenging of the wish, cont'd; Uncle Toby whistles *Lillabullero.* (7) How the green bag was knotted because Obadiah could not hear himself whistle. (8) The knotting of the green bag, cont'd; how this was a link in the concatenation of events against the fortunes of Tristram Shandy. (9) The knotted bag, cont'd. (10) The cutting of the knots; on curses.

(11) The curse of Ernulphus. (12) On exactitude, illustrated by Garrick's *Hamlet;* the inclusiveness of Ernulphus' curse—how all others derive from it. (13) In which Tristram Shandy begins to be born; the midwife's accident; Dr. Slop's "the subordination of fingers and thumbs to ******." (14) A discussion of Dr. Slop's "singular stroke of eloquence" compared to one of Cicero's. (15) Dr. Slop draws from his bag forceps and squirt; Uncle Toby's advantage. (16) Demonstration of the forceps on Uncle Toby. (17) Danger of the forceps mistaking the hip for the head. (18) Lecture on Duration: Walter to Uncle Toby; the chagrin of Walter. (19) The author regrets that the lecture was ended by Walter's petulance. (20) Sleep descends on Walter and Uncle Toby, whereupon the author finds time to write his Preface; the Preface: concerning Locke's favoring Judgment over Wit and how he was "bubbled." (21) How the parlor door hinge has squeaked for 10 years. (22) Rude awakening by squeaking hinges; how heirloom boots became mortars. (23) Tristram Shandy has been born, and Dr. Slop builds a bridge. (24) How this bridge is mistaken for the one destroyed by Trim and Bridget. (25) How the destroyed bridge was to be rebuilt. (26) Return to the "present"; Uncle Toby sends thanks to Dr. Slop for rebuilding the bridge. (27) The enlightenment about the bridge; Walter is led to his room by Uncle Toby. (28) The author shows respect for the tribulations of his father. (29) Man bears pain and sorrow best in a horizontal position. (30) Why Walter's affliction was extravagant: "To explain this, I must leave him upon the bed for half an hour." (31) Discussion between Tristram's great-grandfather and great-grandmother on noses. (32) The same, cont'd. (33) Discussion between Tristram's grandfather and grandmother on noses. (34) Walter's concern with the literature on noses. (35) Walter's collection of this literature. (36) A warning by the author to the female reader. (37) Noses, cont'd. (38) In praise of Hafen Slawkenbergius. (39) Conflict between Walter and Uncle Toby on noses. (40) Locke and noses. (41) Noses, cont'd. (42) Further praise of Slawkenbergius by the author.

BOOK 4

The ninth tale of the tenth decad of Slawkenbergius, translated from the original Latin by the author. (1) Cautious hints concerning the untranslated tenth tale of the tenth decad. (2) Back to Walter Shandy, who is still prostrate. (3) Lashes, metaphorical and literal: Walter Shandy vs. "A grenadier...in *Makay's* Regiment." (4) Trim's memory and his brother in Portugal. (5) A very short aside by Walter. (6) How Walter Shandy rises from his bed of grief. (7) Walter on misfortune.

(8) How "Trismegistus" will counteract a crushed nose. (9) Walter on the laws of chance. (10) The author writes a chapter on "Chapters," while his father and uncle are still on the stairs. (11) The greatness of "Trismegistus": antiphon by Walter and Uncle Toby. (12) How husbands are ignored during childbirth. (13) How the author gets his father and uncle off the stairs at last, as he despairs of ever catching up with the story of his life. (14) Time has truly passed; Walter is awakened by the maid; the leaky vessel carries away "Trismegistus," part of which seeps out. (15) The author writes his chapter on sleep. (16) Walter remains calm. (17) The author's explanation of this calmness. (18) Uncle Toby and Trim regret the misnaming, musing however upon the uselessness of names in battle. (19) The belated Lamentation of Walter. (20) The author on the dangerous and devious turnings of his book. (21) Digression upon kings: how Francis I solved a knotty problem satisfactorily. (22) The author explains that his book is written against nothing but spleen. (23) Walter and Yorick discuss un-naming; Yorick suggests a dinner with learned men. (24) [OMITTED] (25) A chapter has been torn out, and the author explains what was in that chapter: the coach with the erroneous bend sinister in the Shandy arms. (26) The dinner of learned men (The "Visitation Dinner"). (27) The same, cont'd; a misplaced chestnut. (28) Treatment of a chestnut burn. (29) Discussion by the learned men on the naming of a child; how a mother has no relation to her child. (30) On the latter point, between Uncle Toby and Yorick. (31) Walter Shandy's legacy—the ox-moor or Bobby's "grand tour"; how the matter is settled by the death of Bobby. (32) The author: how true Shandeism opens the heart and the lungs.

BOOK 5

(1) The author inveighs against plagiarism; his digression on Whiskers with the story of the Lady Baussiere. (2) Walter is informed of the death of his son Bobby. (3) How Walter carried on: consolation in rhetoric. (4) Containing a choice anecdote: a culmination of Walter's carryings-on. (5) How the author leaves his mother standing outside the parlor door. (6) In the kitchen: a parallel to the parlor declamation. (7) Trim the orator: on Death. (8) In which the author remembers his debt of a chapter on chambermaids and buttonholes. (9) Trim continues: on Death. (10) The same, cont'd. (11) The author remembers his mother outside the parlor door. (12) The author returns to his mother—but does not. (13) What Mrs. Shandy had heard. (14) The matter of Socrates' children cleared up. (15) The author digresses with "Had this volume been a farce...." (16) Walter writes a Tristra-paedia. (17) Tristram has an accident, at the age of five. (18) Susannah confides in Trim. (19)

Digression: Uncle Toby wishes for more cannon; Trim removes the window sashes. (20) Trim champions Susannah. (21) How Trim's succoring Susannah suggests the Battle of Steenkirk to Uncle Toby. (22) The Battle of Steenkirk, cont'd. (23) Susannah, Trim, Uncle Toby, and Yorick advance cn Shandy Hall. (24) The author on his father's variousness. (25) The author mentions his right to go backward. (26) Walter is informed of the accident. (27) Walter finds a certain good in the accident; on circumcision. (28) Walter Shandy: On the Good. (29) A story by Yorick: the battle between Gymnast and Tripet. (30) Walter on the merits of the Tristra-paedia. (31) Tristra-paedia: the origins of society and the rights of the parents (an echo of Bk. 4, Chap. 29). (32) Trim is catechized. (33) Tristra-paedia: Walter Shandy on radical heat and radical moisture. (34) The same, cont'd. (35) The same, cont'd. (36) The same, cont'd. (37) Uncle Toby and Trim on radical heat and radical moisture. (38) The same, cont'd. (39) Dr. Slop delivers a prognosis on the results of the accident. (40) Radical heat and moisture, resumed. (41) The author shouts encouragement and patience to the reader. (42) Another chapter of the Tristra-paedia, on the value of the auxiliary verbs. (43) Auxiliary verbs, cont'd.

BOOK 6

(1) The author looks back at his work and marvels at the quantity of jackasses in the world. (2) The value of the Tristra-paedia: famous prodigies. (3) An altercation between Dr. Slop and Susannah at the dressing of Tristram's wound. (4) A brief statement of events. (5) Walter's conception of the right kind of tutor. (6) The story of Le Fever. (7) The same, cont'd. (8) The same, cont'd. (9) Uncle Toby goes to bed (part of the story of Le Fever). (10) Le Fever dies. (11) The author is impatient to return to his story; however, he takes time to discourse upon sermons. (12) Uncle Toby and young Le Fever. (13) Young Le Fever's military misfortunes; Uncle Toby recommends him as Tristram's tutor. (14) Dr. Slop has exaggerated in public about Tristram's accident. (15) A line on Walter's determination to put Tristram into breeches. (16) On resolutions and Walter's "beds of justice." (17) A historical precedent for the beds of justice. (18) The consideration of breeches in the beds of justice. (19) "Breeches" in the literature of antiquity. (20) The author leaves his characters safely occupied and moves on to another "scene of events." (21) Uncle Toby's battlefield, and (22) the battlefield and the sentry box (several years are telescoped). (23) A town is built for the sake of verisimilitude. (24) About Trim's Montero-cap. (25) The author's encomium to Uncle Toby and Trim; he anticipates Uncle Toby's death. (26) How Trim made the cannons smoke. (27) Uncle Toby's appreciation of Trim's genius.

(28) Uncle Toby fights the temptation of the ivory pipe. (29) The author prepares the reader for love. (30) How all, great and small, have loved. (31) How the peace of Utrecht brings unemployment to Uncle Toby. (32) Uncle Toby's *"apologetical oration"*: in defense of his wishing the war to continue. (33) The author mentions again that he is obliged to go backward and forward. (34) Uncle Toby concludes the peace on his battlefield. (35) A restless peace for Uncle Toby. (36) Disquisitions upon love, to be applied to Uncle Toby. (37) "Let love therefore be what it will, — my uncle *Toby* fell into it." (38) In which the reader himself draws a likeness of Widow Wadman. (39) Mr. and Mrs. Shandy discuss Uncle Toby's amours. (40) The author begins to get "fairly into" his work; lines are drawn to show the reader how he has traveled so far.

BOOK 7

(1) The author prepares to flee from Death; on the low character of Death. (2) The flight: the Channel boat. (3) The choice of three roads to Paris. (4) Should one describe Calais? (5) The author describes Calais. (6) On to Boulogne. (7) Delays on the road; the passengers' speculations on the author. (8) On to Montreuil; the author's patience with French coaches and drivers. (9) Montreuil: Janatone, the innkeeper's daughter, and the transience of her beauty. (10) French post roads and distances. (11) "One gets heated traveling." (12) Abbeville and the inn not fit to die in. (13) On wagon wheels. (14) On Lessius' and Ribbera's estimates of the size of the soul; the author's sense of his death. (15) En route. (16) Reflections on how to pay the post charges and still sleep; the author sees Chantilly (hurriedly). (17) First view of Paris: "So this is *Paris!* quoth I." (18) Enumeration of the streets of Paris, quarter by quarter. (19) En route. (20) How French post-horses are urged on. (21) The above illustrated by the story of the Abbess of Andoüillets. (22) The same, cont'd. (23) The same, cont'd. (24) The same, cont'd. (25) The same, concluded. (26) The author looks back upon the distance he has covered. (27) Trips are interchanged: Tristram's grand tour with his father and his uncle; their visit to the mummies at Auxerre. (28) The author comes to his senses and resumes the first journey. (29) The wrecked coach is sold in Lyons; "Every thing is good for something." (30) "VEXATION upon VEXATION" in Lyons. (31) The story of Amandus and Amanda. (32) The interlude with the ass of Lyons: the author gives "Honesty" a macaroon. (33) Tristram and the Commissary. (34) The same, cont'd. (35) Tristram scores on the Commissary but pays nonetheless. (36) The loss of the "remarks." (37) Back to the

coach-purchaser. (38) The "remarks," used as curl-papers, "will be worse twisted still." (39) Sight-seeing in Lyons: *"Lippius's* clock" and the *"Chinese* history." (40) No tomb to drop tears on. (41) At Avignon: its windiness and its nobility. (42) En route: the author begins to believe that he has outrun Death. (43) The author, while en route, promises the continuation of the story of Uncle Toby's amours; he stops to dance with happy country people; Nannette.

BOOK 8

(1) Further statement on the necessity of going forward and backward. (2) The author expresses confidence in his method of writing a book. (3) The effect of velvet masks on the Shandy lineage. (4) How Uncle Toby finally heard that he was in love. (5) On drinking water. (6) How Uncle Toby's being a water-drinker would have explained Mrs. Wadman's feelings toward him; the author expresses difficulty with this chapter. (7) The author, impatient, points out the care required in telling his story. (8) How Uncle Toby lacked a bed when he first came down to Shandy Hall; how he accepted a bed at the Widow Wadman's. (9) Widow Wadman's nightgowns and cold feet. (10) How Uncle Toby did not learn of her love for him until eleven years later, at the demolition of Dunkirk. (11) The author curses women who don't care whether he eats his breakfast or not; he also curses furred caps. (12) He is struck by his extravagant metaphor. (13) An alphabetical damning of love. (14) How the position of Widow Wadman's house enabled her to attack. (15) The author prefers to be burned from the top down; on the "blind gut." (16) The Attack: Mrs. Wadman and Uncle Toby look at maps in the sentry box. (17) The author treasures a map with their thumbprints. (18) "Dunkirk" is finally destroyed: a continuation of the action first mentioned in Bk. 6, Chap. 34; Uncle Toby is sad. (19) To divert him, Trim essays the story of the King of Bohemia and his Seven Castles; Uncle Toby's argumentativeness. (20) Trim's tale of the wound on his knee and of the fair Beguine who nursed him. (21) The same cont'd. (22) The same, cont'd; Uncle Toby finishes Trim's story for him. (23) Widow Wadman attacks again. (24) How she gets something in her eye. (25) How Uncle Toby does not get it out; a description of Widow Wadman's eye. (26) Uncle Toby breaks a blister and realizes that his wound is not merely skin-deep. (27) Uncle Toby announces to Trim that he is in love. (28) Discussion between Mrs. Wadman and Bridget about Uncle Toby's wound. (29) How a sword gets in one's way. (30) Plans of action by Uncle Toby and Trim. (31) Preparations for Walter Shandy's laugh. (32) Walter laughs; Uncle Toby's blister and Hilarion's ass.

(33) Altercations in the Shandy family concerning love. (34) The same, cont'd; Trim's wager; Walter's letter of advice to Uncle Toby. (35) Uncle Toby and Trim are ready to attack; Mr. and Mrs. Shandy stroll down to observe the campaign.

BOOK 9

(1) Mr. and Mrs. Shandy; her placidity and lack of prurience. (2) Uncle Toby's battle array: how his tarnished gold-laced hat became him. (3) Uncle Toby's fear of the attack. (4) Trim assures Uncle Toby that the Widow Wadman will accept him as readily as the Jew's widow accepted Tom, Trim's brother. (5) The story of Tom and the widow, told outside Mrs. Wadman's house. (6) The same, cont'd. (7) The same, cont'd. (8) Trim and Uncle Toby are seen by Mr. and Mrs. Shandy still standing and talking; the author's sense of the speed of time. (9) The author's comment on the reader's reaction to "that ejaculation." (10) Mr. and Mrs. Shandy await events, as Trim tells his story to Uncle Toby. (11) They agree about the nonsense of fortifications; Mrs. Shandy's agreeableness and Walter's chagrin about the date. (12) The author pauses to balance folly with wisdom to assure the success of his book. (13) The author's method of overcoming dullness while writing; how his laundry bills will prove the cleanness of his writing. (14) The author continues killing time, waiting for Chap. 15. (15) The author realizes that in talking about his digression he has actually made it; his surprise at this fact. (16) Trim and Uncle Toby finally knock at the front door. (17) The front door is opened with great dispatch; the author on finances. (18) [BLANK] (19) [BLANK] (20) Uncle Toby assures Mrs. Wadman that she shall see and touch the very spot where he received his wound. (21) How a woman chooses a husband, illustrated from Slawkenbergius. (22) How all Uncle Toby's virtues are nothing to Mrs. Wadman. (23) Bridget's determination to get the truth out of Trim. (24) The author feels his "want of powers" to continue the story; the Invocation to the gentle imbecile, Maria. (25) In which the author explains the necessity of having written Chap. 25 before he could write Chaps. 18 and 19, which he now presents: *18.* Uncle Toby informs Mrs. Wadman that he loves her; the thanklessness of children and the burden. *19.* Mrs. Wadman's "fiddlestick"; Uncle Toby's confusion and the siege of Jericho. (26) Mrs. Wadman's past concern about Uncle Toby's wound; she asks him where he received the sad blow; Uncle Toby sends for the map. (27) After Mrs. Wadman has put her hand on the spot where Uncle Toby was wounded, the map is sent to the kitchen. (28) Trim explains the siege of Namur to Bridget; her charge and his refutation. (29) Trim learns the

story of Mrs. Wadman's concern from Bridget. (30) How Uncle Toby
and Trim had carried on separate attacks. (31) Trim tells Uncle Toby
of the widow's concern, apropos of her "HUMANITY"; Uncle Toby
is disillusioned. (32) The Shandy family convenes; Walter Shandy on
women's lust. (33) Walter on the "provision...for continuing the race";
Obadiah's child and the Shandy bull; the story about a cock and a bull.

A NOTE ON THE TEXT

Tristram Shandy was written in five installments and published in
these segments:

Book 1 and Book 2	December, 1759
Book 3 and Book 4	January, 1761
Book 5 and Book 6	December, 1761
Book 7 and Book 8	January, 1765
Book 9	January, 1767

The following notes are based on this first London edition, considered
the most authoritative. The quotes preserve the punctuation of this
edition, an important matter because the great use Sterne makes of
dashes gives us a good idea of how *Tristram Shandy* should sound.
These dashes are more effective for his purposes than the standard use
of periods, commas, and semicolons, for as he says, "Writing, when
properly managed,...is but a different name for conversation."

The best edition available to the student is that done by James
Aiken Work (New York: The Odyssey Press, 1940). Work's edition has
a lengthy and perceptive introduction (pp. ix-lxxv), but its most useful
feature for the student — for any reader — is the completeness of the footnotes, which translate the many foreign expressions, identify the many
references that the writer makes to esoteric knowledge and little-known
authors of erudite and specialized texts, provide cross-references to
related matters in the book itself, and function generally as a complete
encyclopedia to *Tristram Shandy*.

SUMMARIES AND COMMENTARIES

BOOK 1

Chapters 1-5

Summary

On the evening of Tristram's conception (the first Sunday in March, 1718), Mrs. Shandy asks a trivial question in the middle of that important event. The irritation it causes in his father has a negative influence on the "animal spirits" which control the makeup of the Tristram-to-be. The foundation has been laid for a "thousand weaknesses both of body and mind" in Tristram.

It was Uncle Toby who told Tristram the story of his conception; he told him also that when Tristram was young, Walter Shandy had observed many things about him that verified his opinion that the trouble had started on that fateful night. Mrs. Shandy, however, never knew or understood the slightest bit of this theory.

Tristram threatens that in telling his story he will not follow any of the rules laid down by the critics, but he realizes that curious readers want to know all the details from beginning to end. He explains that from information he has gleaned from his father's old memorandums, he is able to pinpoint the exact night of his conception. His father was "one of the most regular men in every thing he did"; for example, he wound up the family clock on the first Sunday night of every month, and took care of "some other little family concernments" at the same time – once a month. The one thing and the other were always linked in his mother's mind, hence the question that she asked. He tells the day of his birth (November 5, 1718), and he says that his life has consisted of "pitiful misadventures and cross accidents," just as his father expected.

Commentary

The author makes fun of the "begin from the beginning" novel by giving us the details not of his birth but of his very conception. From the first sentence he established his presence, that of a person with lots of opinions. He is the person and the writer who is the natural outcome of the events that he pictures for us from Chap. 1 onward. The ideas of his father have taken firm hold in his mind, and he is the embodiment of things-gone-wrong. In a way, his book goes wrong from the beginning: instead of giving the reader straightforward facts, he gives minute background and precise explanations about that background. He goes into detail about the details—a propensity that he has obviously inherited from his father.

In addition to establishing his own presence, he shows us without preliminaries his mother and father in bed on that evening. It is as if he has suddenly raised a curtain on the actors who are waiting to begin their performance. At their very first appearance in the book, Mr. and Mrs. Shandy are as vivid and three-dimensional as they are whenever the stage is given over to them, whether for a brief flash or for an extended sequence.

Several important motifs appear in these first chapters. One of them is the Lockean theory of Associationism, introduced in Chap. 1. Two or more ideas become associated in someone's mind; when one of these ideas occurs to him, the other occurs with it automatically. They are inseparably linked. This is a kind of "madness" that periodically springs up in Mrs. Shandy and Uncle Toby, especially in the latter, and naturally they have no control over it. Some of the funniest situations in the book derive from such associated ideas.

Another motif is the author's attention to the believability of his story. Events and conversations that he personally couldn't have witnessed are told to him by someone who was involved, or else he finds documents, letters, diaries which give him necessary facts. That is one of the ways that Tristram remains Tristram and not Sterne as an omniscient narrator.

Still another very obvious motif is the relationship established between Tristram and the reader (sometimes "Sir," more often "Madam"). The reader is always in the forefront of Tristram's consciousness, and not only when he says, "Dear Reader." The reader is made to participate in the book; he finds himself face to face with the author, having questions put into his mouth and supposedly having made comments that the author must answer. Sterne hoped to get the reader to experience the impressions that Tristram writes about, rather than to stand far off and objectify them. The reader was intended not to observe but to participate with Tristram in the re-creation of Tristram's sensations and to reflect upon those sensations as Tristram was reflecting. One could say that Sterne is conducting the reader on a psychoanalytic tour of both Tristram's and the reader's intellectual and emotional being.

The dispersal of the animal spirits is the first of the Accidents that befall Tristram. Its importance can be judged only by what we see in Tristram's character, but if we take Walter and Tristram's word for it, it was an accident with grave consequences.

Chapters 6-12

Summary

The When of his birth having been dealt with, Tristram now promises to go into the How. He hopes, however, that he and the reader will get to know each other better, mainly so that the reader will have confidence in his way of telling his story; he may seem to be clowning, but he asks the reader to give him "credit for a little more wisdom than appears upon" his outside and to keep his temper.

A poor widow who lived in their village was helped with a mid-wife's license by the parson, who paid for it himself as a service to the community. The license is a formal document, overly formal, and the language used in it was the whim of the lawyer Didius. Tristram admits that even the wisest men, "not excepting *Solomon* himself," had their whims and their hobby-horses (i.e., hobbies), and as long as a man "rides his hobby-horse peaceably," it's nobody else's business. Tris-tram has several hobby-horses of his own, in fact. He does feel, however, that important people ("my Lord, like yourself") should do these things in moderation, and he proceeds to write a Dedication to the "My Lord" he has been addressing. The Dedication is brand-new, never offered to anyone before; it is for sale for 50 guineas, and the money is to be paid to him in care of the publisher. All of Chap. 9 and everything relating to hobby-horses is included in the offer; the rest of the book is dedicated to the moon.

The parson who had paid for the midwife's license used to ride about on a "lean, sorry, jack-ass of a horse," even though he owned a very handsome silver-studded saddle. On his horse he was the scandal of the parish and the target of jests and malice. Years before, however, he had owned fine horses, fit for the handsome saddle, but since the nearest midwife lived seven miles away, people in distress borrowed his horse constantly. The result was inevitably a broken-down horse, one after the other. He decided to set up a midwife right there and to ride the same horse—"the last poor devil, such as they had made him... to the very end of the chapter"—in order not to be accused of ulterior motives. But malice is always present, and his parishioners maintained that selfishness and pride were his reasons. The malice persisted to his death ("about ten years ago").

The name of the parson was Yorick, and Tristram says that he was descended from that same Yorick who supposedly was a part of Hamlet's court in Denmark. Yorick was a simplehearted person, innocent in the ways of the world; he was full of jokes and merriment, and he disliked gravity and seriousness. Because of his jokes and the fun he poked at serious people — seriousness, he said, was a *"mysterious carriage of the body to cover the defects of the mind"* — he made powerful enemies, although he could never believe that a joke could make someone hate him. But it was true, and that hate and malice broke his spirit and brought him to an early grave. On his tombstone his dear friend Eugenius had these words engraved: "Alas, poor YORICK!" Passersby who noticed his grave would sigh, "Alas, poor YORICK!" As a tribute to his dear friend Yorick, Tristram inserts a leaf that is completely black on both sides.

Commentary

At this point, Tristram is supposed to begin telling us *how* he was born, but we aren't the wiser about that after these seven chapters. Still, he has asked us to be patient with him as he tells his story in his own way. The midwife and her license are the excuse for introducing the following: 1) Parson Yorick, his character and his troubles, 2) hobby-horses, 3) a misplaced Dedication, 4) the midwife herself, who will eventually assist at the birth of Tristram, and 5) the joke of "Alas, poor Yorick!"

Parson Yorick, one of the major characters of the book, has been seen as a portrait of Sterne himself; the malice directed against Yorick is reminiscent of the personal and political difficulties that Sterne had with some of the important people in church politics in York. The jester in Yorick is in fact very much like the jester in Laurence Sterne, but that biographical information plays no significant part in the construction of the book and we are free to ignore it.

Hobby-horses, introduced quite casually, are the backbone of *Tristram Shandy.* First, we begin to see that Tristram is treating his writing as a hobby: he does it just the way he wants to, and it gives him a lot of enjoyment. Second, everyone of importance in the book has his hobby, and the hobbies are a greater part of their character than is anything else.

The misplaced Dedication shows the liberty that Tristram takes toward the organization of his book. Instead of coming at the beginning, it comes just where and when he wants it. He mocks the concept of dedicating books to great men, underlining the usual financial motive by offering it to anyone who will pay him 50 guineas. This irreverence toward the dignified occupation of novel-writing is characteristic of Tristram, who deliberately breaks whatever rules he can think of. As he discusses the matter, of course, we learn more and more about him — just as he says we would — and we add to what we know of "the life and opinions of Tristram Shandy."

The midwife whose story triggered all this *will* come back into the stream of events, but since the author wants to work in the fable of Yorick the Parson's descent from Yorick the Jester (together with the punch line of the epitaph), the midwife has to wait.

The completely black pages are the first of a series of typographical oddities that sometimes amuse, sometimes put off the reader. They may be considered as personal whims of Tristram, who after all ought to be able to do as he likes with his own book; he includes his doodles and his sketches, and he claims that they are important graphic aids.

Chapters 13-18

Summary

Tristram recalls his duty to continue the story of the midwife so that the reader will remember "that there is such a body still in the world," but again he has other things to say first. One of them is to remind the reader that by "world," he means only "about four or five miles": his village and its environs. He has prepared a map of that world, which is in the hands of the engravers; it will be added "to the end of the twentieth volume." The reader is told this "in confidence," and he is asked not to mention it to the Reviewers.

Apropos of looking something up in his mother's marriage settlement, he says again that there are many things that a man, writing a history such as his, must do as he goes along: "For, if he is a man of the least spirit, he will have fifty deviations from a straight line to make ...which he can no ways avoid." He knows that his story isn't making much headway: "I have been at it these six weeks, making all the speed I possibly could, — and am not yet born." He speaks of his digressions as "unforeseen stoppages...which...will rather increase than diminish," but he intends to keep at it, writing and publishing two volumes of his life every year.

One of the articles in his mother's marriage settlement—quoted in full legal language with Gothic lettering—stipulated that Mrs. Shandy could choose to give birth in London if she desired. A second clause added that if she had some sort of false alarm, she forfeited "the next turn." She had such a false alarm the year before Tristram was born, and Mr. Shandy insisted that she have her child at Shandy Hall when the "next turn" came. He was very angry about the wasted trip, and on the eve of Tristram's conception he told his wife that she was "to lye-in of her next child in the country to balance the last year's journey."

She plans to make the most of it, and since a certain famous obstetrician wasn't available, she decides to have the village midwife. Tristram interrupts (on the day "I am now writing this book for the edification of the world...*March 9, 1759*") to observe that people go from one extreme to the other, illustrating his point by telling of something his "dear, dear *Jenny*" did the other day.

Mr. Shandy, thinking about public opinion in case anything should go wrong with the birth, engages the man-midwife, Dr. Slop, but Mrs. Shandy will have no one but the midwife herself. They finally agree that Dr. Slop will just stand by in case of trouble, and that the midwife will assist at the birth.

Tristram reminds the reader that when he spoke of his "dear, dear *Jenny*," he might have been referring to a daughter or merely to a good friend. A female reader ("Madam") whom he speaks to directly seems to doubt that she is anyone but his "kept mistress." Tristram, however, admits nothing.

Commentary

Tristram says specifically that there is no predictable end to his history of himself; he will simply keep writing until he dies. One reason is that as he writes he is constantly reminded of other related matters that he ought to tell about. This is the "Psychology of the train of ideas," or stream-of-consciousness, which is the common property of all men; one thing reminds him of another, and that reminds him of something else, and so on. (This stream-of-consciousness is not to be confused with the Associationism mentioned earlier, John Locke's name for what he considered a kind of madness.)

All of these related ideas are legitimate material for a *complete* history of an individual, the kind he intends to write. Needless to say, the "story" seems to suffer, but we notice that he always comes around to the point sooner or later. It seems that the writer is deliberately frustrating us, and perhaps he is. But the picture of the writer himself gets clearer and clearer in the meantime, and that is apparently just as important to him.

The author reminds us of what he is doing, in case we don't get the point. Theoretically, he is describing his birth, but after six weeks of writing he is still far from it. The story is kept from advancing not only by such things as the marriage articles and Mrs. Shandy's insistence on the midwife, but also by Tristram's presentation of the man holding the pen: *he* plans so many books, *he* has other stories to tell, *he* knows a girl named Jenny, *he* tells the reader that a Platonic relationship is possible between himself and Jenny, and so on. He gives specific dates (i.e., he is writing Bk. 1 on March 9, 1759) that are real only for himself; all the other characters are dead by then.

One question that comes up regularly is this: Is what Tristram has to say about himself as important as the story that he interrupts? The answer to this can come only after the reader has finished the book. Another question is this: Does Sterne actually expect to finish his book, does he, like Tristram, plan to go on and on indefinitely? One possible answer to this latter question is that the reader comes to see how impossible it is *ever* to exhaust the thoughts and opinions of an individual; in saying that he expects to go on publishing two books a year for life, Tristram (and Sterne) is saying that completeness and endings are purely relative ideas. Whenever he stops, the book will be finished in a certain sense; and in another sense, it can never be finished.

Everything has relevance so far. We begin to see that Yorick's horses, the midwife's license, the marriage article, the man-midwife (Dr. Slop) are all part of the chain of events leading up to Tristram's birth. The nose that was destined to be squeezed flat is explained by each of those facts.

Tristram's "dear, dear *Jenny*" and the innuendo of her relationship to Tristram is another part of his character. Sexuality, serious and non-serious, is woven into the fabric of the story; although there is a constant suggestion that it is hopelessly bungled and unsatisfactory, it is a basic element in their lives — as in all life.

We see Walter Shandy's hobby beginning to unfold in these chapters. It consists of Theories and Hypotheses. Walter will hold forth by the hour, orating on one subject after another, throughout the book.

Chapters 19-20

Summary

With regard to Walter Shandy's insistence on certain ideas (such as his theories about the politics of France in the preceding chapter), Tristram tells about his father's Theory of Good and Bad Names and his skill in argument. When he had a particular notion, Walter Shandy "would move both heaven and earth, and twist and torture every thing in nature to support his hypothesis." One of his theories was that the child's name influenced his fortunes: *Trismegistus* and *Archimedes* were powerful names, *Simkin* and *Nick* were deadly names ("*Nick*, he said, was the DEVIL"), *Jack*, *Dick*, and *Tom* were neutral and worthless.

"But, of all the names in the universe, he had the most unconquerable aversion for TRISTRAM." "Who," asks Walter, "ever heard tell of a man, call'd *Tristram*, performing any thing great or worth recording?" "TRISTRAM...was unison to *Nicompoop*." Tristram calls the reader's attention to the title page of his book, and he asks us to sympathize with his father.

Addressing his female reader again, Tristram asks her "How could you...be so inattentive in reading the last chapter?" After he sends her back to reread and find the point where he said that his mother was not a Catholic, he moralizes to the rest of his readers about people who skip the "deep erudition and knowledge" in a book and read only "in quest of the adventures."

When his female reader "returns," Tristram points out what she should have seen, and he then quotes the "Memorandum presented to the Doctors of the Sorbonne," a lengthy medical-legal-ethical document in French; the document deals with the question of whether a child can be baptized in the mother's womb by means of a small syringe. Tristram has an alternative suggestion: baptize all the "HOMUNCULI" at one time in the father "by means of a small syringe."

Commentary

The dual nature of Walter Shandy's hobby-horse is portrayed: his theories and the oratory with which he tries to convince people of his theories. The most important thing in the world to Walter is a Hypothesis; *everything* takes second place to it. He is a man with a ruling passion, dominated by one of the Humours. He is the source of some of the subtle but rollicking comedy of *Tristram Shandy:* Walter has his theories, but no one can understand them but him. He never convinces anyone of anything, but he never stops trying. He will go to any lengths to persuade; he is as eloquent as any of the great orators of antiquity, and he instinctively knows all the tricks of elocution and delivery. But nobody is ever persuaded.

His Theory of Names is obviously a setup for another frustration: Tristram's Third Accident (the second is to his nose). Walter hates the name *Tristram* above all other names, and yet his son comes to be named *Tristram*. This fact of course provides us with a laugh, but it is also easy to see that Tristram has a purpose in introducing to us Walter's theory — even though he hasn't been born yet.

Pulling the reader into his work and sending her back to find out where he made a particular statement, Tristram has the excuse of defending his book again: it is not an adventure story, and the reader who misses a point misses something valuable. He is exaggerating grossly the importance of the point (and he knows he is): it was very trivial, and the reader could not have seen it beforehand. But he is still right, i.e., he wasn't sending her off on a wild-goose chase technically.

He now therefore has the further excuse for introducing a piece of "learned jargon," a bit of arch-trivia about intrauterine baptism. Like Yorick, he is always against gravity and seriousness; he intends to ridicule and satirize the "Learned Doctors of the Sorbonne," the Catholic authorites, and he does so by reducing the suggestion to an absurdity.

Even though Tristram sees through his father's weakness, in this matter he shows himself to be very much the son of Walter Shandy, using the kind of argument that Walter himself might have used.

Chapters 21-25

Summary

As Mrs. Shandy begins to go into labor, Walter and Uncle Toby are sitting in the parlor. Walter wonders what all the noise is upstairs, and Uncle Toby says "I think — ."

Tristram interrupts to say that before he can let him finish his sentence, it is appropriate to outline Uncle Toby's character. Writing on "this very rainy day, *March* 26, 1759, and betwixt the hours of nine and ten in the morning," he recalls that none of the Shandy females had any character except his great-aunt Dinah. Then Uncle Toby's character drawing goes on. Toby was a most virtuous, extremely modest man; he acquired his modesty from "a blow from a stone...at the siege of *Namur*, which struck full" upon his groin—a long and interesting story. " 'Tis for an episode hereafter." In the interim, suffice it to say that whenever Walter told the story of their Aunt Dinah, who "was married and got with child by the coachman," Toby's sense of modesty was outraged. Walter persisted in expounding his theory of their family: "What is the character of a family to an hypothesis?" he would say, and because it was useless to argue with him, Toby would whistle *"Lillabullero,"* a favorite song. After outlining the classical types of argument, Tristram suggests that this kind of argument be named the *"Argumentum Fistu-latorium"*—argument by whistling.

Tristram discusses his digressions, noting that in his latest one, "there is a masterstroke of digressive skill": as he was about to tell of Toby's character, he thought of his Aunt Dinah and the coachman, but the reader will "perceive that the drawing of my uncle *Toby*'s character went on gently all the time,...so that you are much better acquainted" with him now. Thus, he concludes, "my work is digressive, and it is progressive too, — and at the same time."

Digressions are the sunshine, the life, and the soul of reading, says Tristram, "Take them out of this book for instance, — you might as well take the book along with them." The author's problem is serious: if he digresses, the whole book stands still, "and if he goes on with his main work, — then there is an end of his digression." But he has constructed the book so that, like one wheel within another, the "digressive and progressive movements" go on together, and "it shall be kept a-going these forty years."

If people had windows in their breast, we could tell at a glance what someone was like. But they don't, and we are liable to make many mistakes about their character. To avoid these errors, Tristram says, "I will draw my uncle *Toby*'s character from his HOBBY-HORSE." It was an unusual hobby-horse, but before telling what it is, Tristram must first explain how Toby came to acquire it.

After being wounded in his groin, Toby was confined to bed for four years; since there was so much brotherly love between them, Walter took him into his house in London. Talking about the circumstances of his wound gave him much relief, so Walter gladly listened to his stories of the siege in which he was hurt. Something came up, however, that threatened to retard his cure. What it is, Tristram will tell about in the next book; the reader can't possibly guess.

Commentary

Although we aren't told it quite yet, Tristram actually has brought his mother to the point of bearing him. But it is to be put off still. Uncle Toby's character is the next item on the author's agenda, and he launches into it by interrupting Toby's sentence. (That sentence will be completed 10 chapters later, Bk. 2, Chap. 6.)

Again we have a reminder that the writer has his own thoughts — it is March 26, 1759 — and one of his thoughts is about his Aunt Dinah, a family scandal. The story of Aunt Dinah and the coachman serves to show the great difference between the brothers, Walter and Toby, and it shows Toby's extreme modesty.

Tristram analyzes his "digressive-progressive" technique, and his argument in its favor is clear and convincing: the digressions are really digressions, but the story goes on because, as he says, we continue to know more about Uncle Toby's character even though Tristram is ostensibly talking about something else.

His discussion of the way he has solved the problem is a piece of learned jargon; he is satirizing techniques, rules, and mechanical approaches to writing. But it is nonetheless true; his claim that the digressions work in much more closely than they seem to turns out to be so. The architecture of the whole labyrinth is very careful. The supposedly casual attitude he has to his forward development — he'll be writing the book for 40 years — is just a typical Shandean joke; he knows where he's going, and he has a sense of proportion.

The character drawing goes on. The wound in Toby's groin starts his hobby, although what it is we don't know yet. An exposé of Toby's hobby will provide all the clues we need in order to understand his character, but the author must first give more background about the origin of the hobby. But before that, he must tell about something before that — in the next book.

BOOK 2

Chapters 1-5

Summary

The "perplexities" that threatened to retard the healing of Uncle Toby's wound consisted of the difficulty of explaining clearly the technical details of where and how he received the wound; he would "oft times puzzle his visiters, and sometimes himself too."

He thought of getting a "large map of the fortifications of the town and citadel of *Namur*." He did so, and that was how his hobby got started.

Tristram thinks about certain objections that will be made by the critics, and he answers their charges. He reaffirms that his book is a history. "Of who? what? where? when?" "It is a history-book, Sir,...of what passes in a man's own mind." He cites John Locke's *Essay Concerning Human Understanding*, pointing out that Locke's interpretations do *not* apply, and he says that Uncle Toby's "life was put in jeopardy by words," not by ideas.

Toby gets his map and studies it. He learns more and more about fortified towns (like Namur) and begins to study all manner of military writings on military architecture, ballistics, trajectories, projectiles. Tristram fears for his uncle's health, and he urges him — as if he were actually there at that moment — to give it up: "Intricate are the troubles which the pursuit of this bewitching phantom, KNOWLEDGE, will bring upon thee.... Fly — fly — fly from it as from a serpent.... O my uncle! my uncle *Toby!*"

Tristram tells why he ended the chapter at the "last spirited apostrophe" (it was for the sake of letting it "cool"). Good writers must consider these matters of emphasis and proportion.

Uncle Toby gives up the study of projectiles and turns to the "practical part of fortification only." He begins to long mightily for his recovery, although we don't know yet what he has in mind. Tristram will tell us in the following chapter what Toby has in mind, and after that, " 'twill be time to return back to the parlour fire-side, where we left my uncle *Toby* in the middle of his sentence."

The wound begins to heal nicely, so Toby and his servant, Corporal Trim, embark for Shandy Hall in the country. The reason is that Toby's bedside table was too small to hold all his books and apparatus. When he asked Trim to order him a larger table, Trim suggested that they go to Toby's estate near Shandy Hall; there, under Uncle Toby's expert direction, he would construct on the lawn scale models of the fortifications, complete in every particular so that "it should be worth all the world's riding twenty miles to go and see it." Uncle Toby blushed with joy at the idea, and they are off on his hobby-horse.

Tristram says that the history of their campaigns will make an interesting "underplot in the...working up of this drama," but later. "At present the scene must drop, — and change for the parlour fire-side."

Commentary

The author ties together all the facts leading up to and including Uncle Toby's hobby: the setback in his getting well, the first idea for a map of Namur, the military books that fire his imagination, Trim's proposal for the scale models on the bowling green at Shandy Hall, and their setting off to start work. We know all there is to know about that part of Toby's character, and henceforth, when Toby sees everything in relation to that single ruling passion for fortifications, we understand perfectly.

Tristram's references to John Locke again remind us that the author was working in the context of eighteenth-century psychology, philosophy, and epistemology. Even though he cites Locke in order to show a contrary notion, he depends quite a bit on Locke.

The author's continuing close involvement with his characters and his insistence on his job as author is seen in the "spirited apostrophe" to his Uncle Toby and his beginning a fresh chapter. In Chap. 4 he remembers the interrupted sentence — although we may have forgotten it already — and at the end of Chap. 5 he tells us that later he will pick up what is digression (Toby's hobby) and make it a part of the main story. The suspension of the story of Toby's hobby is as calculated as the suspension of Toby's sentence.

Corporal Trim's character is also drawn by means of his hobby-horse: "The fellow lov'd to advise, — or rather to hear himself talk.... Set his tongue a-going, — you had no hold of him." The proposal by Trim to build the models is a perfect demonstration of his oratory;

he is involved with Uncle Toby in the fortifications, but that is merely a second-string hobby-horse for him.

Chapters 6-14

Summary

"I think," said Uncle Toby, "it would not be amiss, brother, if we rung the bell." They then learn that Mrs. Shandy has begun labor; Mrs. Shandy has sent Susannah for the old midwife, and Walter sends Obadiah for Dr. Slop (who lives eight miles away).

In answer to Walter's question as to why Mrs. Shandy insists on having the old midwife when an expert obstetrician is available, Toby says, "My sister, I dare say,...does not care to let a man come so near her ****." Tristram points out the beauty of those four asterisks; it is impossible to say whether Toby added a word or left the sentence as given above.

Walter considers the idea ridiculous and says so. Toby demurs, pointing out that he knows practically nothing about women, and he alludes to the "shock I received the year after the demolition of *Dunkirk*, in my affair with the widow *Wadman*; — which shock you know I should not have received, but from my total ignorance of the sex." As Walter is about to tell his brother about the "right end [and] the wrong" end of a woman, there is a loud rap at the door.

Tristram says that "it is about an hour and a half's tolerable good reading since my uncle *Toby* rung the bell, when Obadiah was order'd to saddle a horse, and go for Dr. *Slop*." (He is referring to what happened – although we didn't see it – when he interrupted Toby's sentence in Bk. 1, Chap. 21.) The critics might say that it has been only "two minutes, thirteen seconds, and three fifths" – referring to the moment when Tristram actually does tell us the end of Toby's sentence (two short chapters back), and Obadiah is sent off on the eight-mile trip to fetch Dr. Slop. If the critic insists that Obadiah could not have gotten there and back already, then Tristram concedes that actually Obadiah met Dr. Slop "three-score yards from the stable-yard"! The doctor was coming by "merely to see how matters went on."

Tristram asks the reader to "imagine to yourself" Dr. Slop, a "little, squat, uncourtly figure of a Doctor *Slop*, of about four feet and a half perpendicular height," knocked off his little pony into the mud by

Obadiah, who comes charging around the corner of the stable on his big coach horse.

Walter and Toby are astounded to see him, the former measuring in his mind the very short time elapsed since he rang the bell to send off Obadiah. The same phenomenon instantly brings into Toby's mind "*Stevinus,* the great engineer." Tristram promises to explain why, "but not in the next chapter."

Writing is like conversation, says Tristram: you leave your partner something to imagine. Imagine, then, he says, Dr. Slop all cleaned up and changed. But Dr. Slop has left his bag of obstetrical instruments at home. Obadiah is dispatched again to get them.

Toby tells Dr. Slop that his "sudden and unexpected arrival" reminded him of the great Stevinus. Walter bets that Stevinus is a writer on fortifications, and so he is. Toby lectures Dr. Slop about military terminology until Walter expostulates with him about his lack of feeling for Mrs. Shandy's "pains of labour." "I wish the whole science of fortification, with all its inventors, at the devil."

Toby does not take offense; apropos of his gentleness, Tristram observes that "my uncle *Toby* had scarce a heart to retaliate upon a fly," and he tells the Story of Uncle Toby and the Fly. Once, he caught an "over-grown" fly which had "tormented him cruelly all dinner-time," and he put it out the window saying, "Go poor devil, get thee gone, why should I hurt thee? — This world surely is wide enough to hold both thee and me." Tristram learned "one half of [his] philanthropy" from that event.

Toby's good nature moves Walter to beg his pardon, and the brothers are tenderly reconciled.

Walter, by the way, announces that the conception of children (i.e., the sexual act) doesn't give him much pleasure.

Toby picks up the subject of Stevinus again; that famous engineer had built a wind-propelled "sailing chariot" that traveled on land. Dr. Slop's improbably-speedy appearance seemed to be due to such a contrivance. Dr. Slop has himself seen the machine in Holland, and he points out its superiority over horses, "which...both cost and eat a great deal." Walter begins his Theory of Economics but is interrupted by the opening of the door.

Commentary

Tristram really has gotten us back to Toby's interrupted sentence and back to the parlor.

The battle about "midwife vs. Dr. Slop" goes on, and Toby takes Mrs. Shandy's side. His statement about Mrs. Shandy's modesty provides Tristram with the excuse for a bawdy joke: did he or didn't he intend a word after the sentence? These are jokes for Tristram, and they might also be jokes for Walter, but not for Toby. When he alludes to "widow *Wadman*" and his "shock," we know nothing about that yet; it will be the major part of the plot of Bks. 8 and 9. But if we remember then the things that Tristram is telling us now about his uncle, we will have full insight into the event and its consequences.

The mention that Toby makes of the affair with Widow Wadman underscores Tristram's time-scheme: Tristram is being born this evening, Toby refers to the shock that he received five years before, the novel ends with the events leading up to that shock and its aftermath — five years before Tristram was born.

Tristram again makes fun of critics and rules for writing novels — unity of time and place, in particular. It is diabolically clever, the way he has imposed two periods of time on Obadiah's going for Dr. Slop: the one and one-half hour stretch between Bk. 1, Chap. 21, and Bk. 2, Chap. 8, and the two minutes and thirteen seconds between Bk. 2, Chap. 6, and Bk. 2, Chap. 8. Either could work, depending on whether or not a critic actually brought up the matter; as it happens, the critic does bring it up, so Tristram resolves it by explaining that Dr. Slop was just outside. Tristram is constantly busy out-thinking and outwitting everybody.

The description of Dr. Slop on his pony and the collision with Obadiah is a masterpiece of figure-drawing; every gesture and movement is described with jewel-like precision. We know that Sterne was an amateur artist, and Tristram says the same about himself in the first mention of hobby-horses. Visual description is a constant element in the book; minute details are given so that we see what is going on.

When Toby is reminded of Stevinus, we have another example of "mad" Associationism: Dr. Slop must have come in a wind-driven machine like Stevinus'. Tristram manipulates the Stevinus motif the way he did the interrupted "I think — ": he leads up to it and backs away, teasing us with it before finally telling us the why of the association in Toby's mind.

The episode of Uncle Toby and the Fly has always been a favorite. Many people who reject *Tristram Shandy* as too chaotic, too bawdy, or too dull cherish this story among others. The story illustrates the eighteenth-century doctrines of Benevolence and Sentimentalism: the tender emotions of the reader are awakened by such gentleness and delicacy of feeling. It was physically constructive and healthful to experience and participate in such tenderness and goodness. Fortunately, Uncle Toby is such a *truly* good character with other interesting and delightful traits that we don't see him as a one-sided goody-goody. Earlier readers were quite content to interpret him in that light, however. The writer of the book enjoys his own delicate sensibility (i.e., sensitivity) and his responses to those delicate emotions. At the same time, however, he (both Tristram and Sterne) suggests in a subtle way that it is somewhat phony, exaggerated, and superficial: note, for example, how Toby speaks to the fly—"I'll not hurt a hair of thy head." After all, it's a *fly*. This will be called the First Delicate Story. Nevertheless, Toby's goodness is touching and real, and it is easy to share William Hazlitt's opinion that he is "one of the finest compliments ever paid to human nature."

Two more of Walter's Theories never get told: On the Right and Wrong Ends of a Woman, and On Economics.

Chapters 15-19

Summary

Corporal Trim enters with the copy of Stevinus' book, which Toby had sent him after. Toby tells the Corporal to take the book back home, but first Walter jocularly asks him to look through the book for a "sailing chariot." As Trim shakes the book, out fall some papers which turn out to be a sermon. Walter asks Trim to read some of it, and he is delighted to have the chance to perform. Walter asks Dr. Slop if he objects; he doesn't, saying "it may be a composition of a divine of our church" (the Catholic church). Trim says that since it is on Conscience, "'Tis wrote upon neither side."

Tristram describes in fine detail the Corporal's stance, the position of his legs, the angles of his body, etc.; he has the posture of an expert orator.

The way Trim reads the first sentence of the Sermon provokes Dr. Slop into an argument with the others: *"For we* trust *we have a good Conscience."* Dr. Slop defends the Inquisition, which would persecute anyone who took exception to the text of the Bible, and Trim tearfully speaks about his brother who has been imprisoned by the Inquisition for 14 years.

Trim continues reading, with comments by both Dr. Slop and Walter on the meaning of the sermon. It turns out to have an anti-Catholic bias, and Dr. Slop falls asleep in the middle. Toward the end, in a description of the practices of the Inquisition, Trim takes the sermon literally as an account of what is happening to his brother Tom, and he cannot read without commenting at each line. Walter finishes the reading.

The sermon, they decide, was written by Parson Yorick, who had borrowed Toby's copy of Stevinus and left the sermon between the pages.

Obadiah returns with Dr. Slop's bag of instruments, and Walter informs Dr. Slop that he is to be merely an auxiliary; unless the midwife sends for him, he is to remain downstairs. Dr. Slop says that there have been such improvements in obstetrical knowledge, especially in "the safe and expeditious extraction of the *foetus,"* that he wonders "how the world has——" and he is interrupted by Uncle Toby, who says "I wish...you had seen what prodigious armies we had in *Flanders."*

Tristram in turn interrupts, dropping "the curtain over this scene for a minute." There are two things to say which he should have said 150 pages ago; after that, the scene will continue.

First, he reminds us of his father's character, referring us to what we learned about him from his Theory of Names. Then he tells us of Walter's elaborate *"Shandean* hypothesis"—supported by references to many learned authorities—that the most important center in the brain is the medulla oblongata. This part of the head is during birth "compressed and moulded into the shape of an oblong conical piece of dough, such as a pastry-cook generally rolls up in order to make a pye of." To protect his child's brain, Walter suggests to Mrs. Shandy that she have a Caesarean delivery; "but seeing her turn as pale as ashes at the very mention of it,...he thought it as well to say no more of it."

The next best thing to protect his child's medulla oblongata is Dr. Slop and his "new-invented forceps." They will act as armor against the medulla's being compressed like the pastry-cooks' pie dough.

Tristram asks the reader to conjecture about how Uncle Toby got his modesty from a wound upon his groin, how Tristram "lost" his nose because of the marriage articles, how he came to be called "TRISTRAM" in opposition to his father's hypothesis, and "fifty other points." But the reader will never unravel these mysteries by himself; he must be content to wait for "a full explanation of these matters till the next year."

Commentary

The insertion of the Sermon on Conscience is somewhat artificial; it was one of Sterne's sermons, a popular one, and he felt it would provide good reading even in the context of *Tristram Shandy*. But the use that he puts it to is in complete harmony with the story. The occasion that it provides for the arguments between Walter and Dr. Slop and the emotions it provokes in Corporal Trim make it an organic part of the novel.

Tristram leaves us suspended with Uncle Toby's wish about our seeing the "prodigious armies" in Flanders. It will turn out to be another demonstration of Toby's childlike reasoning — direct and very simple. The interruption in which Tristram outlines his father's theory about the brain and his trust in Dr. Slop's forceps is important; we know that it will play a role at the right time, and we suspect that since it is a cherished theory of Walter's, something is going to go wrong.

Before ending the second volume, Tristram tells us what we still have to find out, matters that he has raised but not resolved yet. This final paragraph functions like a "cliff-hanger"; the interested reader will be sure to buy — and read — the next installment.

In this last chapter there is a strange and very interesting footnote that has a most important function. Apropos of the title of a "learned" work on childbirth, we find this at the bottom of the page: "The author is here twice mistaken.... Mr. *Tristram Shandy* has been led into this error" by such and such — more learned jargon. Laurence Sterne, the author of the novel, is pretending to be merely the *editor* of Tristram Shandy's Life and Opinions, putting distance between himself and "Mr. Tristram Shandy." There are two or three other such footnotes, and they remind us — Sterne wants us to know — that the person doing the "internal" writing is not Laurence Sterne, but Tristram Shandy.

Summary

Uncle Toby repeats his wish about their seeing the "prodigious armies" in Flanders, but nobody sees the point. Dr. Slop is so dumfounded that Walter steps in to question the purpose of the wish: "— What prodigious armies you had in *Flanders!*" And as he says that, he removes his wig to mop his brow. He removes his wig with his right hand and reaches for his handkerchief with his left hand. Unfortunately, the handkerchief is in his right-hand pocket.

He twists and wiggles, trying to reach his right pocket with his left hand, and the "transverse zig-zaggery" reminds Toby of a maneuver at Namur. He is about to send Trim for the map, but a look at Walter's face dissuades him. Instead, he sits patiently until Walter somehow manages to get the handkerchief.

Walter begins again. At one time people were content if children managed to be born any which way; they paid no attention to the danger to their brains. Toby rejects the idea that the dangers are greater now than before and that people were all born with damaged brains merely because the forceps had not been invented.

Commentary

Toby's "wish" was an anticipation of Dr. Slop's hobby-horse notion that forceps were the answer to everything; Dr. Slop was about to say that he didn't understand how people managed to get born, and Toby said that the armies in Flanders had many men in them. His common-sense attitude stands out in sharp contrast to both Dr. Slop's and Walter's fixation about the delicacy of the brain; he whistles "Lillabullero" when Walter suggests that people born naturally, without help of forceps, are mentally defective. Uncle Toby obviously thinks faster than we give him credit for.

The scenes in which Walter reaches for his handkerchief with the wrong hand may seem to be merely humorous trivia; they are that, but they serve another important purpose as well. All he had to do was put his wig back on his head, take it off with his left hand, and take his handkerchief from his right pocket with his right hand. But not Walter

Shandy. This is the physical counterpart of his intellectual gymnastics: everything is twisted around as needed to fit in with his hypotheses, and once he sets out with his left hand, he intends to succeed. Somehow he manages to, but the process is unnatural, Tristram suggests.

Walter's movements are described so that we can imagine every second of the contortions and feel the ridiculousness of the situation.

Chapters 7-12

Summary

Dr. Slop is cursing Obadiah heartily. Because the bag of instruments jingled so that he couldn't hear himself whistle, Obadiah had tied the drawstrings of the bag into great knots. The knots are elaborate; furthermore, he has "tied and cross-tied them all fast together from one end" of the bag to the other. Tristram observes mournfully that if there had been a fair contest between his delivery from his mother and the delivery of the green bag from its knots—if both "she and Dr. *Slop* both fairly started together"—his mother would have won "at least by twenty *knots*," and his nose would have been saved. Dr. Slop was aware of that fact.

As Dr. Slop wrestles with the knots, he gets angrier and angrier. He cuts them with Walter's penknife, cutting his thumb at the same time. He curses Obadiah still more vigorously. Walter teases him about his great curses over such a small thing as a cut thumb, and when Dr. Slop says that no curse is too great, Walter hands him a ready-made curse to read, provided he reads it aloud. Dr. Slop, suspecting nothing, takes the curse, which turns out to be a form of "excommunication of the church of *Rome*...write by ERNULPHUS the bishop." Uncle Toby whistles "Lillabullero" as Dr. Slop begins. When he realizes what it is, he tries to get out of the reading. Walter holds him to his agreement, and Dr. Slop reads the powerful curse, inserting the name "Obadiah" at the proper points.

Tristram tells us his father's hypothesis that all modern curses and oaths derive from Ernulphus' anathema.

Commentary

The chain of events working against Tristram has another couple of links forged for it in these chapters. Little things conspire against him,

have always done so; little things of course conspire against every one of
the Shandys, but sometimes they are at cross purposes. The knotting of
Dr. Slop's bag—for the triviality of allowing Obadiah to hear himself
whistle—worked against Walter's and Dr. Slop's plan for having the
forceps handy for the delivery to protect the child's brain. And the
cutting of the knots, freeing the forceps and making them available for
the delivery, worked against Tristram's nose (as we shall see later).
Everything *seems* to be dictated by pure chance, and yet everything
goes uniformly wrong.

Walter's collection of esoteric literature serves him well for a
change: when he baits Dr. Slop into using the Catholic excommuni-
catory curse, Dr. Slop is caught in his own trap.

Chapters 13-20

Summary

The midwife, having slipped and hurt her hip, sends for Dr. Slop.
He tells Uncle Toby that by means of "******," everything will turn
out all right for the Shandy family.

Tristram praises Dr. Slop's "******"—actually, a pause—pointing
out that when you have the thing about you, it is more effective to produce it than to name it. Dr. Slop is searching around in his bag for it,
and when he pulls out the forceps, the forceps pull out a syringe. Uncle
Toby takes his advantage and says, "Good God!...*are children brought
into the world with a squirt?*"

In a demonstration of the forceps, Uncle Toby's hands are skinned,
and "you have crush'd all my knuckles...to a jelly." Walter wishes that
Dr. Slop would extract the child by his feet rather than by his head.
Discussion follows between Dr. Slop and the midwife about which part
of the foetus is showing, his hip or his head. Walter and Dr. Slop talk
about the dangers to both parts from the forceps; "When your possibility has taken place at the hip,—you may as well take off the head too,"
Walter says glumly.

Time has passed and Walter and Toby are sitting in the parlor alone.
Walter is about to lecture on Duration, when Toby takes the wind out of
his sails by giving the exact answer to Walter's rhetorical question. To
Walter's chagrin, Toby doesn't understand it at all and he isn't interested
in understanding it. Conversation ceases.

Tristram feels that the loss of Walter's conjecture "upon TIME and ETERNITY" is a great one: "by the ashes of my dear *Rabelais,* and dearer *Cervantes,*" it was a "discourse devoutly to be wished for!"

Walter and Toby, gazing at the fire, fall asleep. Everyone is accounted for, sleeping or busy elsewhere. Tristram now has a moment to spare, and he writes his Preface. The Preface, lengthy and full of Shandean extravagance, deals chiefly with Locke's Wit and Judgment; like the knobs on the back of his chair, they go together. Locke—and anyone else who shares his view—was wrong to think that the one (Judgment) was more important than the other.

Commentary

Events continue to conspire against the child: Dr. Slop has been called into service with his forceps. We get some idea of the dangers facing the babe from the demonstration on Toby's clenched hands and the discussion of hips and heads.

The author toys again with rhetorical devices, using asterisks to catch our attention and giving Toby the chance to make fun of Dr. Slop and his forceps. The beginning of Chap. 14 shows the author's skillful use of omission; we figure out from Uncle Toby's complaint about his skinned hands and crushed knuckles that a demonstration has taken place.

The Lockean concept of Duration, which Walter pompously and elaborately paraphrases, is that "men derive their ideas of duration from their reflection on the train of ideas they observe to succeed one another in their own understandings." It is a basic part of Tristram's method of presenting his story; together with the "psychology of the train of ideas," it enables Tristram to break away from the conventional scheme of temporal and spatial reporting.

Again, Toby squelches Walter's oratory. Although Tristram says he regrets the loss of the discourse, he is being ironic: Walter's learned jargon is no better than that of the many other authorities that Tristram pokes fun at.

The mention of Rabelais and Cervantes points up their importance to the author; there are many references to both of these writers' works, and there are paraphrases, parodies, adaptations, and skillful imitations of some of their stories and motifs scattered throughout *Tristram Shandy.*

Although it was once a popular thing to accuse Sterne of plagiarism, close examination will show that whatever ideas he borrowed, he reworked so that they are uniquely his own.

When Tristram says "All my heroes are off my hands," and he is finally free enough to write his Preface—another misplaced item—we have the Stage Director completely undisguised. Although he pushes them around gently, has them go offstage, or makes them go to sleep, he manages to give the impression that they are real individuals who are capable of getting in his way and thwarting his plans.

His Preface, intended as a corrective to Locke's preference for judgment over wit, shows his continued involvement with philosophical matters. Tristram is on his own business, talking to the more intellectual members of his audience; the Shandys and their problems have been put aside.

Chapters 21-30

Summary

For ten years, Walter resolved to have the parlor-door hinge mended: three drops of oil would have done it. Tristram (who hasn't fixed it yet) resolves to do it within his own lifetime.

Corporal Trim has been making model mortars for the fortifications, and he proudly carries them to the parlor to show them to his master. The squeaking hinge wakes up Walter, who is distressed to find that to make the mortars, Trim has cut off the tops of a pair of heirloom boots. He is pacified, however, and "brought into perfect good humour with them in an instant" when Toby says that all of his concern with the fortifications is "for the good of the nation."

Trim tells them that Dr. Slop is in the kitchen, "making a bridge." Toby says, "Tell him I thank him heartily." But Toby is mistaken about what the bridge is, and in order to explain that, Tristram says he must tell about something that should really come in later. He explains the problems of digression again: if he waits till later, "I ruin the story I'm upon,—and if I tell it here—I anticipate matters, and ruin it there." He calls on the "POWERS" to set up a guidepost to show a poor author which way to go.

When Uncle Toby began to court Widow Wadman, Trim courted her maid, Bridget. But when Toby ceased courting his paramour, Trim continued to meet his on the sly for five years. One evening, shortly before the night of Tristram's birth, Trim met Bridget and decided to show her the fortifications by moonlight. Somehow the little Dutch drawbridge "was crush'd all to pieces that very night." Walter has been teasing Toby and Trim ever since; Toby believes it to have been a simple accident (Trim slipped and they both fell on the bridge) and thanks providence that "the poor fellow did not break his leg," but Walter borrows Toby's military metaphor and speaks of the power of Trim's artillery.

They set out to build a new bridge but can't decide on the proper model — for current military and political reasons. Toby thinks that one type with a lead weight in "eternal ballance" may be just the thing; but it is "cycloid" in shape, and he doesn't know enough about cycloids. So "the bridge went not forwards. — We'll ask somebody about it, cried my uncle *Toby* to *Trim.*"

When Trim announced that Dr. Slop was making a bridge, Walter is about to begin teasing and baiting them again. "*Trim*'s answer, in an instant, tore the laurel from his brows, and twisted it to pieces": " 'Tis a bridge for master's nose. — In bringing him into the world with his vile instruments, he has crush'd his nose...as flat as a pancake to his face...." " " — Lead me, brother *Toby*, cried my father, to my room this instant."

Tristram feels melancholy about his father's misery, and it makes his writing more sober and serious. "A tide of little evils and distresses has been setting in against" his father, and "now is the storm thicken'd, and going to break, and pour down full upon his head."

Man bears pain and sorrow "(and, for aught I know, pleasure too)" best in a horizontal position, and Walter throws himself face down across his bed. His posture is in every detail that of a man "borne down with sorrows"; the knuckles of his left hand are "reclining upon the handle of the chamber pot." Toby sits quietly in a chair at the opposite side of the bed.

Although any man would be distressed at "the breaking down of the bridge of a child's nose, by the edge of a pair of forceps," Tristram must explain why his father was so extravagant in his grief. To do so, "I must leave him upon the bed for half an hour, — and my good uncle *Toby*...beside him."

Commentary

Among the lesser evils that plague Walter is the squeaking hinge that always disturbs his naps; his involvement with great projects and theories and his absolute incompetence in dealing with little matters is one of the ironies of his character. His son, Tristram, isn't very much different: although he sees the irony in his father's incompetence, he has obviously inherited the inability to cope with small problems.

Toby's illusion about the importance of his hobby is funny, but our laughter at it doesn't obscure the inherent humanity and altruism in his character. Walter and Toby's love for each other is shown several times, not only in Walter's ready forgiveness about the heirloom boots but also in Toby's sympathy with Walter's shock about Tristram's nose.

The problems of story and digression are again dealt with, and our understanding of Tristram's method grows with his discussion of the choices he has to make about when to introduce parts of his story. His comments about the helplessness he feels serve to underline his techniques.

These techniques are undeniably effective. When we analyze the order of story and digression, we find this arrangement of cause and effect: a bridge is mentioned; Toby mistakes the bridge, we are told; Toby has courted Widow Wadman and Trim had courted Bridget; Trim continued his courtship, although Toby discontinued his; the draw-bridge was destroyed in Trim's courtship; Walter teased Toby and Trim about the destruction of the drawbridge; Toby doesn't know enough about the new bridge he intends to build; Dr. Slop is "making a bridge"; Walter begins to tease again; the bridge is for a smashed nose. Each of the antecedent events needs to be told if we are to know the entire situation. The accumulation of these events makes the whole story far more profound than it could be otherwise; and because the author tells us what he is "forced" to do in order to present that story, we escape the boredom we might otherwise feel.

Forward-pointing as well as recapitulation of past events is important: again Tristram mentions Uncle Toby's courtship of Widow Wadman, promising still again that he will tell that story later. And he will tell it, in every detail, in the last two volumes of the book.

The shattering of Walter's hopes is very funny—because he is caught in his own teasing—and also very poignant. Tristram feels

48

compassion for his father, but he is always able to laugh, at himself and at his own difficulties as well as at others. He'll laugh at Walter's hand resting on the chamber pot (shortly), and that is one of the justifications for his describing Walter's position with the eye of a painter and a poet.

Having gotten his father to the point of grieving over Tristram's nose, the author must now take an extended tour backward to explain.

Chapters 31-42

Summary

Tristram's great-grandfather is forced to settle upon his great-grandmother a jointure ("widow's portion") of 300 pounds a year, even though her entire dowry was a mere 2,000 pounds. The reason she insisted was that he had "little or no nose."

By "nose," Tristram says that he means *Nose,* "nothing more, or less." If there are two senses, they are like two roads, one dirty and the other one clean; "Which shall we take?" is the question Tristram asks the reader to decide for himself.

His great-grandfather signed the agreement. The great-grandmother outlived not only her husband, but her son also—by 12 years; and her grandson, Walter Shandy, had to pay her the 300 pounds a year during all that time. All because of short noses. It is easy to understand Walter's prejudices against short noses, says Tristram. "He would often declare...that he did not conceive how the greatest family in *England* could stand it out against an uninterrupted succession of six or seven short noses." Again Tristram tells the reader not to let his fancy carry him away: "I mean the external organ of smelling, or that part of man which stands prominent in his face."

Walter becomes obsessed with noses and his opinions on the subject are very important to him. He collects every book and treatise on the subject just as Uncle Toby did on military architecture.

Tristram pays homage to his Uncle Toby. He speaks with great love of his character, and he vows that Toby's fortifications "shall never be demolish'd."

Walter was fortunate to get a copy of Bruscambille's prologue on long noses. He solaced himself with it the way "your worship solaced yourself with your first mistress, — that is, from morning even unto night." Then he got hold of other learned works on the subject, above all, that of the "great and learned *Hafen Slawkenbergius*," of whom Tristram will soon write.

Walter was disappointed in Erasmus' writings "upon the various uses and seasonable applications of long noses," and Tristram warns the female reader to behave "like *Tickletoby*'s mare" in keeping Satan from getting "astride of your imagination."

The unlearned reader must read, says Tristram, if he (or she) wants to know who Tickletoby's mare is and what the other learned references in his book are, and especially if he wants to understand the significance of the marbled page that follows immediately.

Walter struggles with the sense of Erasmus' "celebrated dialogue," but only by scratching the words with a penknife can he get the sense he wants out of it: "See, my dear brother *Toby*, how I have mended the sense. — But you have marr'd a word, replied my uncle *Toby*. — My father put on his spectacles, — bit his lip, — and tore out the leaf in a passion."

Tristram invokes Slawkenbergius, who knows all about noses, and asks where his (the latter's) genius came from, what his inspiration was. With him he compares the other authorities, Prignitz, Scroderus, Ambrose Paraeus, and their theories. The theory of the last one "overthrew...the system of peace and harmony of our family," and started a great dispute between Mr. and Mrs. Shandy.

The cause? "My mother, you must know, — but I have fifty things more necessary to let you know first." Among them, there is his father still lying across the bed; he promised he "would go back to them in half an hour, and five and thirty minutes are laps'd already." And there is, very important, "a tale out of *Slawkenbergius* to translate."

The difference between Walter and Toby is again illustrated, this time by Walter's trying to explain Slawkenbergius to his brother. Toby resists all efforts to make him understand; even the great Locke would have despaired at making him comprehend the matter.

Walter persists, but since he unfortunately uses the word "siege," Toby's fancy takes a "short flight to the bowling-green" and his fortifications. When Walter speaks of the "ingenuity these learned men have all shewn in their solutions of noses," Toby asks, "Can noses be dissolved?" Again Walter loses his patience. For Toby, the only reason that "one man's nose is longer than another's" is that "God pleases to have it so." When Walter replies that "there is more religion" in Toby's answer "than sound science," Toby whistles "Lillabullero."

Walter believes that all civilization could be reconstructed from Slawkenbergius' "rich treasury of inexhaustible knowledge," and although Tristram doesn't consider it with the same reverence as his father, he admits that he likes the "tales," and he promises to tell the reader "the ninth tale of his tenth decad."

Commentary

In these chapters we are introduced to Walter's theory of noses, and we begin to learn why noses are so important to him. Thus, when Tristram's second Accident occurs—his smashed nose—we have the perspective against which to measure its importance. Noses also furnish him with the opportunity to tease the reader about the latter's salaciousness; although Tristram constantly denies that he has ulterior motives in talking about noses, if the reader insists that Tristram has, then the responsibility for the sexual interpretation is the reader's. Tristram believes that he is revealing us to ourselves.

One of the most successful elements in the book is the feeling it imparts to us that the writer is talking about a real family, the sense of involvement that the writer has with these people. It establishes Tristram as an individual apart from Sterne; the tribute to Uncle Toby in Chap. 34, the love of the nephew for his generous, warm-hearted uncle, is moving and it is appropriate to the "I" who is always before us. We may remind ourselves again that *Sterne* had no Uncle Toby, and although some commentators have found clues to Toby's character in Sterne's father, that is really beside the point.

The many references to the "learned men" who wrote about noses —some of them real writers and real texts—make another sizable block of learned jargon at which Tristram pokes fun. It is all meat and drink to Walter Shandy, but Tristram keeps his sense of proportion and understates his amusement at his father's obsession. In Walter's "research" into the meaning of Erasmus' dialogue—his literally scratching the letters with a knife to change their shape (and consequently the meaning of the words)—we see another proof of his lack of proportion about his "theories"; it seems that he will do anything to make his point. Toby, who knows nothing about abstract reasoning, looks at everything with the clear sight of an innocent child; he knows only that in order to prove his point, Walter has changed a word.

The store of Rabelais' sexual allusions is again tapped so that Tristram can tease the reader. Whether this reference is made for its own sake or whether Tristram actually wants to educate the reader is a constant question.

A story within his digressions — why his mother and father fought about something — is interrupted because there are more important digressive matters to go into. Tristram's control of the story is again obvious: most readers will find that they had forgotten about Walter when Tristram reminds them that 35 minutes have passed since the time he said that he would come back to Walter in half an hour. Tristram isn't quite ready to get back to his father; the tale from Slawkenbergius comes first.

Toby's question, "Can noses be dissolved?" stimulated by Walter's speaking of "solutions of noses" while his brother was distracted, is considered to be one of the funniest lines in English literature; the complete absurdity of the question, however, gives a sort of perspective to Walter's point. The question is actually no more absurd than the basic premise that it is worthwhile to write treatises about noses.

BOOK 4

Chapters 1-14

Summary

Tristram tells the tale from Slawkenbergius' "great book." On facing pages, he presents the "original Latin" (for several pages): a stranger with a *very* large nose passes through the town of Strasburg and sets the townspeople on their ears. The people are aflame with curiosity about him and about his nose; all of his gestures are carefully noticed and commented upon. He mutters to his mule and refers to an unfortunate affair with "Julia." Among others, many nuns are troubled and stirred up by the sight of his nose. Learned men in Strasburg comment at great length on the nose. The tale, after furnishing the occasion for a discussion of Luther and his theology, ends with the encounter between the long-nosed stranger (Diego) and the brother of Julia, who has been pining away with love for Diego.

The tenth tale of Slawkenbergius, the one following the tale that Tristram has just translated, is a masterpiece, Tristram tells the reader. He merely hints at its contents, leaving the reader (the lady reader) eternally in doubt as to whether the stranger's nose was a true one or a false one.

Walter has been lying across the bed for an hour and a half. He wiggles his toes and stretches his hand—the one lying across the handle of the chamber pot. When he realizes what it is, he gives a "hem!" and raises himself to his elbow. The sight gladdens Toby's heart. When Walter rhetorically asks, "Did ever a poor unfortunate man...receive so many lashes?" Toby answers, "The most I ever saw given...was to a grenadier, I think in *Makay*'s regiment," and Walter collapses again upon the quilt.

A discussion follows between Toby and Corporal Trim about the whipping of the grenadier in Makay's regiment, who Trim contends was innocent. Trim's good nature is shown by the tears he sheds at the memory of the injustice; Toby weeps also. Toby tells Walter that he has left Trim his bowling-green in his will, and Walter smiles; Toby then tells him that he has also left Trim a pension, and Walter looks grave.

Tristram records the attitudes and positions of his father in getting up from the bed; attitudes are important because they are the "resolution of the discord into harmony, which is all in all." Walter rises and addresses his brother about the misfortunes that afflict man. In his simple fashion, Toby believes that God will take care of everything, but Walter points out that that is no solution: man carries his share of counteracting and undoing misfortune. In order to "set my child's nose on" (Religion "makes every thing straight for us," Toby says), "He shall be christened *Trismegistus*," says Walter. Toby piously hopes that that will do the trick.

As they walk down the stairs, Walter comments on the incredible laws of chance which accounted for the forceps breaking his child's nose; Toby points out that it could have been worse: "Suppose the hip had presented" itself. Walter agrees.

Tristram tells about the chapters he has been planning to write, and he wonders how he will ever get them all done. He tells about his capriciousness, how he ends a scene when he has something else to do —just as he has now left his father and his uncle upon the stairs in order to write his Chapter on Chapters.

Still on the stairs, Walter tells Toby what a great man Trismegistus was. Susannah rushes by; Walter inquires about his wife and the child, but Susannah is gone in a flash. Commenting upon the burden that women have in bearing children, Toby says "God bless them" and Walter says "Devil take them" simultaneously.

How can he get his father and his uncle off the stairs. Tristram asks the help of literary critics about how to proceed. And while he is on the subject of needing help, he points out that after writing for a year, he is in the middle of his fourth book and has just gotten to the point of telling about his first day of life (and not even that). He worries about the slow progress of the book: he has 364 days more to write about than when he started. How will it ever get finished? Obviously he will be writing all the rest of his life, and there is no hope of ever catching up: "I shall never overtake myself." "Heaven prosper the manufacturers of paper," he wishes, because there are going to be many volumes of *The Life and Opinions of Tristram Shandy!*

Somehow his father and Uncle Toby have gotten down the stairs.

Because the child is apparently expiring, Susannah runs to Walter's room to ask what name he should be baptized with before he dies. He tells her *"Trismegistus,"* but he doubts that she can remember the name: "Thou art a leaky vessel, *Susannah,*...canst thou carry *Trismegistus* in thy head, the length of the gallery without scattering?" She is off like a shot, with Walter trying to find his breeches so that he can make sure she gets the name right. She has a headstart, however, and when she tells the curate that the name begins with "Tris — ," he says that it must be *"Tristram"; "Then 'tis Tristram-gistus,"* she insists. There is no such name, insists the curate (his name also happens to be Tristram). The child is baptized, "and so *Tristram* was I called, and *Tristram* shall I be to the day of my death." Walter arrives and asks the curate if Susannah remembered the name. The curate, "with a tone of intelligence," assures him that she did, and Walter goes slowly back to bed.

Commentary

With much restraint, Tristram plays peek-a-boo with the reader in his tale "translated from Slawkenbergius"; the answer to the question, Does the author have a dirty mind? must come from the reader. The tale is suggestive without a doubt, but the humor and the exaggeration are much more important than the symbolism. No one today would feel that he was "sidling up and whispering a nasty story," as Thackeray said of him last century. Bawdy is bawdy, and no one would deny that Tristram has a sizable streak of bawdiness in his makeup. We are not shocked by the facts of life, however, in these decades, and we are more capable of seeing the expression of those facts as part of the character of Tristram. The satire on philosophical and theological pedantry is fully as important to the writer as the nose symbolism, and to read it primarily as a bawdy tale is to read it with at least one eye closed. Further, Tristram is at work here to see what the reader will admit to himself about himself.

Tristram returns to his father on the bed, reminding us again that he has forgotten nothing. The humor of Walter's hand lying across the chamber-pot handle and his chagrin about it put the gravity of the situation into perspective: the crushing of his child's nose isn't so very serious except that Walter thinks it is.

Toby's literalness — one of his dominant traits — again knocks Walter down; the metaphor of man receiving lashes means nothing to Toby. Lashes are lashes, and he knows someone who received a far greater number of them than Walter.

Sentimentalism — the quality that supposedly makes man better because of the tender feelings he experiences — runs riot in the scene where Toby and Trim discuss the injustice of the whipping. Both are very much moved by the remembered scene, both shed tears. Tristram seems to have a sense of proportion about the value of sentiment; just as his father has: Walter approves of Toby when the latter says that he is leaving his fortifications to Trim because of Trim's good heart, but Walter feels that Toby is carrying sentiment too far when he says that he is leaving Trim *money* as well. Sentiment shouldn't cost anyone anything, in Tristram's and Walter's understanding of it.

Tristram explains again the importance of describing the details of a person's posture: the reader learns much more about an individual in that way. This basis for the analysis of Tristram's people is the same as the hobby-horse; everything a person is interested in, together with his posture, gestures, and mannerisms, helps us to understand what he is truly like.

The third Accident is about to take place: the misnaming. Tristram has prepared us for this as far back as Bk. 1, Chap. 19, where he tells us his father's theory about names. Here we see how much Walter is banking on the name as an antidote to the smashed nose, and we will be prepared for his disappointment when he learns of the misnaming. To make matters even worse, there is false consolation in Toby's reminding Walter that if the child's "hip" had been grabbed by the forceps, he would have regretted it much more. The "hip" too will have its turn (later), and Walter will have a chance to do more lamenting.

Tristram discusses his authorial difficulties again, telling us that it isn't easy to write a book like his. How do authors manage to introduce unrelated chapters? How can an author express himself on a subject which isn't in the least related to his "story"? We see how Tristram does it: he merely goes ahead and does it; and in pointing out the apparent lack of unity, he shows us what Tristram and his book are like—different from everyone else. The difficulty in getting his father and uncle down the stairs has a moral to it: other writers just drop a curtain on the scene, and the reader takes for granted that everything worked out as it was supposed to. But this writer wants us to see that nothing happens by chance. The writer has the responsibility of taking care of every detail, and if he is to do his job well, he can't take the easy way out. We see the author doing his work and explaining it to us as he does it.

He raises the problem again of catching up with his life: if a life is to be the subject of a book, mustn't all of it be written down for the reader? Obviously it cannot. The question that the reader will ultimately ask himself is whether *Tristram Shandy* was finally finished, and the answer will probably be Yes and No both. At any rate, the question is an interesting one, and the picture of the writer desperately trying to catch up with himself is a piquant one. We can say that he knows of the problems as well as we do—or, better, he makes us aware of what he knows —and that too is part of the individuality of this writer.

When Susannah comes for the name of the child, and Walter tells her "Trismegistus," we know already what is going to happen. One can almost believe in the unfortunate destiny of the child. Nobody works *for* Walter; everyone works against him. Susannah almost gets the name right—"Tristram-gistus"—but the ignorance of the curate swings the balance in the wrong direction: he had simply never heard of the name.

Shandean humor—i.e., things aren't really as funny as they seem— predominates. Walter, falsely reassured about the name, goes back to bed. Does Walter believe that everything is all right?—he goes *slowly* back to his bedroom.

Chapters 15-22

Summary

Tristram writes a Chapter on Sleep — apropos of the fact that everyone is asleep — and he sticks to the subject.

Walter asks Susannah to send "Trismegistus" down so that he and Toby can see him. The request touches off a general panic: Susannah confesses that the child has been named "Tristram," and Mrs. Shandy is in a "hysterick fit" about it. Walter calmly puts on his hat and goes out.

Tristram explains why his father went out to the fish pond with this latest affliction instead of taking it upstairs to the bed as before: first, it was different, and second, there is something about fish ponds.

Trim enters and tells Uncle Toby that "it" wasn't his fault — meaning the cow's breaking down the fortifications (first mentioned in Bk. 3, Chap. 38) — and Toby reassures him that it was the fault of Susannah and the curate — meaning the misnaming of Tristram. They agree that names don't mean very much in the long run, i.e., in the heat of battle: Trim would have fought as gallantly under his own name (James Butler) as he did under his nickname. They are acting out a valiant offensive when Walter re-enters. He seats himself and begins his Lamentation: everything has so far gone wrong for his child, but the name "Trismegistus" might have fixed it all: conception, infelicitous gestation period (because Mrs. Shandy "fumed inwardly" about not being able to go to London to have the baby), pressure on the skull by being born head first, crushed nose. Toby recommends sending for Parson Yorick.

Tristram considers the charge of a critic (his usual accuser) that he has trampled on many people with his horse (i.e., his hobby-horse, the book he is writing), even on a king. He denies it and tells the story of King Francis I of France. The King, hoping to make friends of the Swiss, offers them the honor of being godfather to his latest son; when they want to name the child "*Shadrach, Mesech,* and *Abed-nego*" — all three — the King demurs. Since there is no money in the royal treasury to buy them off and soothe their feelings, the King decides to go to war with them.

The author says that he is ashamed to ask the reader to take him seriously now after his "fanciful guise of careless disport," but seriously, he is not writing against King Francis I or against any of a host of other things. "If 'tis wrote against any thing, — 'tis wrote, an' please your worships, against the spleen," that is, against bad humor. His intention is to "drive the *gall* and other *bitter juices* from the gall bladder, liver, and sweet-bread of his majesty's subjects...down into their duodenums."

Commentary

Although a chapter on Sleep contributes nothing to the Shandy family story, it is valid from the point of view of the author himself: he is writing a book that contains "various things" besides Shandy history. The chapter is outside the Shandy history but inside the "Life and Opinions" framework.

The third Accident is revealed to Walter as he discovers that there is no one in his house named "Trismegistus." The author skillfully varies the impact of this latest frustration; it is a grave blow to Walter, but he doesn't comment until several chapters later when he unburdens himself of his Lamentation. In the meantime we remain in suspense, wondering why he doesn't react immediately and what he will do when he does react.

Misunderstanding and faulty communication surge up still again when Trim and Toby discuss the "accident," Trim thinking of the cow and the fortifications, Toby, of the misnaming. We are reminded of the "bridge" of Bk. 3.

There is nothing but hobby-horses in Chaps. 18 and 19: Trim and Toby are caught up by their enthusiasm about how one breaches a fortification, and Walter enters deep in thought about all the awful things that have destroyed the future of his child.

Should we take Tristram seriously when he says that the main purpose of his book is to amuse and cheer up the reader? We can easily believe him, but we should not limit our understanding of it to just that point; here he says only that he is writing *against* spleen. He is writing it *for* many other things. The difficulty lies in believing that anyone who can find humor in practically everything can ultimately have serious things to say as well. A serious manner — "gravity" — is *"a mysterious carriage of the body to cover the defects of the mind,"* quotes Tristram earlier (Bk. 1, Chap. 11). Levity and humor, similarly, may be covering up something too — something other than "defects of the mind," of course.

Chapters 23-32

Summary

Walter Shandy and Parson Yorick discuss the possibility of renaming the child. The only way they can find out for certain is by discussing the matter thoroughly with the learned church lawyers and divines. They will do this at a dinner, and Toby will go along.

Tristram has torn a chapter from the book (Chap. 24), and he explains what was in it and why he did it. It contained a description of the journey on horseback of Walter, Toby, and Trim to the dinner.

The family coach has a coat of arms with a bend sinister (a bar indicating that the family has a bastard in its origins)—painted in by mistake but thus far uncorrected. Walter refuses to ride in a coach "carrying this vile mark of Illegitimacy upon the door," and he decides that they will travel by horse. The description of that journey, says Tristram, is "so much above the stile and manner of any thing else I have been able to paint in this book, that it could not have remained in it, without depreciating every other scene." Proportion is most important: "be but in tune with yourself, madam, 'tis no matter how high or how low you take it." The risk of inserting the missing chapter is this: "A dwarf who brings a standard [yardstick] along with him to measure his own size...is a dwarf in more articles than one."

Kysarcius and Didius expostulate with Parson Yorick because the latter cut up his sermon—the one he had just delivered—and lighted his pipe with it (the Dinner is over and they are sitting around the table eating roasted chestnuts and smoking). Yorick explains that because of the trouble he had in composing that sermon, he is taking his revenge on it. Phutatorius exclaims "Zounds!" at that point, and Uncle Toby thinks that the oath signifies that he is about to attack Yorick. He is wrong, however: a hot chestnut has fallen from the table into Phutatorius' open fly without his noticing it, and the heat has finally gotten through to him. He manages to draw it forth and throw it to the floor. When Yorick picks it up—he considers "a good chestnut worth stooping for" and that one "not a jot worse for the adventure"—Phutatorius is convinced that Yorick had somehow managed to drop the chestnut into his breeches. Thus, Yorick has another enemy.

A discussion follows on the best treatment for a chestnut burn, "for one would not apply to a surgeon in so foolish an affair," says

Phutatorius. The conclusion is that a "soft sheet of paper just come off the press" is best: the dampness of the paper, the "oil and lamp-black with which the paper is so strongly impregnated" will do the job. "You need do nothing more than twist it round," advises Eugenius. It happens that the second edition of Phutatorius' book *On Keeping Concubines* is just coming off the press; the company, however, advise him not to use the paper from *that* book.

The Learned Men get to work on the problem of Tristram's name. They discuss the cases in which baptism would be invalid. Getting off onto other subjects, they bring up the point that legally, *"the mother is not of kin to her child."* They discuss at length the case of the Duchess of Suffolk, found by the law courts to be unrelated to her son and therefore not able to inherit his property. Toby is about to whistle "Lilla-bullero," but he desists when Walter begs him not to.

The discussion of Tristram's naming comes to nothing, and even though Walter was "hugely tickled with the subtleties of these learned discourses," he is as unhappy as before about Tristram's name. A legacy of a thousand pounds, left to him by his Aunt Dinah, raises his spirits and distracts him for a while. But then the question of what to do with the money begins to weigh on him. Many projects occur to him, the final two being whether to clear a large piece of land—the Ox-moor—or to send his older son, Bobby, on a tour of the Continent (a tradition in the Shandy family). On the one hand, the Ox-moor, which had already cost him a good deal in original purchase price and in a lawsuit, would produce a good income when cleared, cultivated, and planted; on the other hand, Bobby was entitled to the advantages of travel.

Walter cannot decide which course to take and he would have "certainly sunk under this evil...had he not been rescued out of it...by a fresh evil." The matter is solved for him by the death of Bobby.

Pointing out that he is heir-apparent from this time forward because of Bobby's death, Tristram says that this is where his Life and Opinions should have begun. He renews his complaint about how many things have to be written about; therefore he names this his Chapter of Things, and he promises a Chapter on Whiskers the very first chapter of his next volume—"in order to keep up some sort of connection in my works." He regrets that he has not yet been able to get to the "choicest morsel" of this work: the story of his Uncle Toby's "amours." He assures the reader, however, that when he finally does tell that story, it will redeem the entire book. He mentions his "dear Jenny" (that is "the thing to be *concealed"*), and he reaffirms his earlier statement about the physiological value of his book: "True *Shandeism*...opens the heart and lungs,... forces the blood and other vital fluids of the body to run freely thro' its channels, and makes the wheel of life run long and chearfully round."

He takes his leave, promising to present the next installment in a year, "(unless this vile cough kills me in the mean time)." It will present a story "you little dream of."

Commentary

The "torn-out chapter" (Chap. 24) is another reminder of Tristram's craftsmanship, his intention to control what goes into his story, where it goes, and what relationship it should have to the whole work. Although he is exaggerating in his usual tongue-in-cheek way, we have no reason to consider it just a joke. He often speaks of the details of writing with frequent reference to reputable authorities, and the principle he says he is following — that of being "in tune," consistent, in his writing — is certainly a valid one. He pokes fun at himself in speaking of his writing as that of a dwarf (rather than a literary giant), but he is clever enough to know that the outstanding passage would make his average production seem less valuable. This thesis is convincing, even if we don't believe he really had written and then torn out a passage. He is a purposeful author, and he wants his readers to know that he is. The entire business is just another problem a writer has, and Tristram is always asking himself the question he presents in Bk. 4, Chap. 10: "Is a man to follow rules — or rules to follow him?"

The family coach with the "bend sinister" is another instance of how little things don't get done, no matter how irritating they are. The painting out of the erroneous line would require little more effort than the "three drops of oyl with a feather" to remove the squeak from the parlor door. But Shandys tackle only big problems.

The dinner of the Learned Men (the "Visitation Dinner") is presented *in medias res,* and somewhat past that point. The men have met, have eaten, and are just about to begin their discussion, a discussion that bears no fruit, offers no consolation to Walter. Although the fine legal points delight Walter, especially the case which proves that the mother and her child have no legal kinship, the basic problem remains unsolved. Tristram makes fun of the pedantry that makes such a contention, and he puts it into perspective by showing its effect on Uncle Toby, the literal-minded man who asks what the Duchess of Suffolk had to say about the decision that her son was not related to her.

The chestnut burn offers the occasion for another piece of bawdiness, and the learned men (including Yorick and Eugenius) exercise their wit in discussing remedies.

Walter Shandy is always Walter Shandy, and when he is rescued from his dilemma of what to do about Tristram's name by the legacy, he is immediately back on the horns of a new dilemma: clear the Ox-moor or send Bobby on a trip. As we see shortly, indecision is so painful to him that he is grateful for any solution, regardless of the consequences.

Tristram again indulges his fancy in holding a carrot before the horse—the reader—by only mentioning Bobby's death. But the trick keeps us going forward until we come at last to the details. He takes seriously the business of "some sort of connection" in his work; Bobby's death will carry us over to the next installment, just as will the promise of a Chapter on Whiskers (whatever that might be!). The most important promise, however, is the story of Uncle Toby's "amours": that is what kept the eighteenth-century reader afloat. He will finally keep that promise too. Whether it is the "choicest morsel" of the book is for the reader to decide, but it is worth pointing out that if a book such as this depends on one "choicest morsel" for its justification, it probably isn't a very important book. The best thing is to consider this as another Shandean statement and put it in its place next to all the Shandean characteristics that make up the book.

This final chapter of Bk. 4 is designed to hook the reader: the author lists the things that he intends to do as a bridge between the present section and the forthcoming ones, he coyly says that he will continue to say nothing about his "dear Jenny," he reminds the reader that humor is the basic justification for his book because it keeps the reader healthy by stimulating the "vital fluids" in their appropriate functioning, and he promises him an extraordinary story if he will read the next installment.

(The "vile cough" that he warns may kill him in the meantime does finally kill Laurence Sterne in 1768, a year after the ninth book of *Tristram Shandy.*)

BOOK 5

Chapters 1-14

Summary

A wild coach trip somehow makes Tristram think of a story he had read, and he tries manfully to avoid using that story in his book as if it were his own. He fails, however, and we get the Fragment upon Whiskers. Although he regrets having promised the reader a Chapter on Whiskers, he keeps his promise.

The ladies in waiting of the Queen of Navarre discuss the charms of certain of the gentlemen of the court. Their having or lacking whiskers becomes the chief criterion of their excellence (having them is better than not having them). "Whiskers" takes on a subtle significance, and one of the women, the Lady Baussiere, is obsessed with the idea to the exclusion of everything else. "The word in course became indecent, and...absolutely unfit for use," and there the story ends.

Walter Shandy is busy measuring distances on a map and calculating the cost of Bobby's trip on the Continent (to be financed by Aunt Dinah's legacy), but he has a hard time because of the frequent interruptions of Obadiah. A letter is brought in, and Walter asks Toby to read it. It bears the news of Bobby's death.

Tristram cites authorities who affirm "that it is an irresistable and natural passion to weep for the loss of our friends or children," but Walter "managed his affliction otherwise." Eloquence is Walter's consolation, and Tristram explains by recounting an incident: Walter owned a "favourite little mare" which he had Obadiah take to be bred with "a most beautiful Arabian horse" in order to produce a good riding horse for his personal use. He looked forward eagerly to this prize offspring, but "by some neglect or other in *Obadiah*, it so fell out, that my father's expectations were answered with nothing better than a mule, and as ugly a beast of the kind as ever was produced" (another little Shandy accident!). Everyone expected Walter to slaughter Obadiah. But it turned out otherwise: "See here! you rascal, cried my father, pointing to the mule, what you have done! — It was not me, said *Obadiah*. — How do I know that? replied my father." Walter is delighted with the chance to make that remark: "Triumph swam in my father's eyes, at the repartee — ...and so *Obadiah* heard no more about it."

Eloquence and witty repartee make up for many things, and Bobby's death gives Walter the chance to make an oration about death and the fall of civilizations. He goes on and on, and poor puzzled Toby is his captive audience. Then, in one of his stories he mentions the word "wife." At that moment, Mrs. Shandy happens to be passing the parlor door, and the word "wife" — "a shrill, penetrating sound of itself" — comes through even more clearly because Obadiah had left the door slightly open. She stops instantly, puts her ear to the door, and listens "with all her powers." Tristram says that he must leave her in that position for "five minutes" in order to tell what has been going on in the kitchen.

The Shandy household is a "simple machine," but, says Tristram, it has "all the honour and advantages of a complex one": "Whatever motion, debate, harangue, dialogue, project, or dissertation, was going forwards in the parlour, there was generally another at the same time, and upon the same subject, running parallel along with it in the kitchen." After Obadiah brought in the letter to Walter, he left the door ajar — ever so little — so that he could hear what the letter was about. "Before my father had well got over his surprize, and entered upon his harangue," Trim is about to speak on the same subject in the kitchen. This system of "communication," Tristram observes, saved "my father the trouble of governing his house." Tristram intends to compare Walter and Trim as orators on the topic of death, "two orators so contrasted by nature and education, haranguing over the same bier."

The announcement by Obadiah in the kitchen — "My young master in *London* is dead!" — brings a variety of responses: Susannah sees herself acquiring her mistress's colorful wardrobe (since Mrs. Shandy will go into mourning), the "fat foolish scullion" is grateful that she is not dead, and Obadiah himself laments about the work he will have in clearing the Ox-moor (the alternate candidate for Aunt Dinah's legacy). Trim orates on the fleeting quality of life: "Are we not here now," he says, striking the floor with his cane, "and are we not — (dropping his hat upon the ground) gone! in a moment! — " "'Twas infinitely striking," Tristram says admiringly, and the eloquence with which Trim dropped the hat should be a lesson to all men: "Meditate — meditate, I beseech you, upon *Trim's* hat."

Tristram interrupts himself to recall to the reader that in the previous book he had promised a "chapter upon *chamber-maids and button-holes.*" He has been advised against it, however, because "the two subjects, especially so connected together, might endanger the morals of the world."

Trim continues: "Is not all flesh grass? — 'Tis clay, — 'tis dirt," and everyone "looked directly at the scullion — the scullion had just been scouring a fish-kettle. — It was not fair. — " " — What is the finest face that ever man looked at!...what is it! (*Susannah* laid her hand upon *Trim's* shoulder) — but corruption? — *Susannah* took it off." Death, says Trim, is nothing, but it is best to die on the battlefield;

each of the servants has his idea of where and how it is best to die. The kitchen cabinet concludes its session with Trim about to recount the story of Uncle Toby and Lieutenant Le Fever (to be told later in Bk. 6, Chap. 6).

The author remembers that he has left his mother eavesdropping at the parlor door, but before he lets things go forward, he points out that any woman would have been similarly captured by hearing her husband mention the word "wife," particularly in the context that follows. Walter is working the "abstract of *Socrates*'s oration" into his long lament, and he closes with "I have three desolate children" (says Socrates). "— Then, cried my mother, opening the door, — you have one more, Mr. *Shandy*, than I know of." "By heaven! I have one less, — said my father, getting up and walking out of the room."

Toby explains that "they are *Socrates*'s children," and he leads her to Walter for the rest of the explanation.

Commentary

The introduction to Bk. 5 contains a witty joke about plagiarism: the author suggests that he is unable to resist the temptation to borrow from other people's work, but at the same time he pretends to speak harshly about such borrowings. Part of the joke lies in his declaiming against plagiarism, using borrowed language. Both Tristram and Laurence Sterne are jokers, and it often seems that a borrowed passage was inserted to see how many readers would raise a hue and cry about it. The fact of the matter is this: Sterne *used* everything. Whatever he borrowed took new shape, new direction, and new meaning from the molding power that he exerted on almost everything that came under his hand. Whether the change derived from rearrangement of the components or from mere setting them in his own context, it is always impressive for the insight it gives us into the mechanics of his creative genius. Writing for an urbane and widely read audience, he could not have expected to fool them; we can safely assume that he knew his readers would recognize what he had borrowed and that he gave them credit for seeing the point of the borrowings. No one cried plagiarism until 25 years after his death — another and a different generation. And during the Victorian era, all critics felt morally obligated to chastise Sterne for his unacknowledged borrowings, even though some of these critics commented at the same time on the skillful and creative use to which he put those few passages.

Like the sections on Noses (end of Bk. 3 and beginning of Bk. 4), the Fragment on Whiskers is full of bawdy innuendo; and just as he pointed out that if the world wanted to consider the nose as an indecent symbol, it was the world's responsibility, so he says the same thing about whiskers. There is nothing that is exempt, nothing too farfetched to be considered in two senses, one of them sexual.

Chapters 2 to 14 demonstrate Tristram's intricate planning. A series of causes and effects interrelate these chapters and lead up to one splendid punch line: Obadiah brings the letter with the news of Bobby's death; he leaves the door open a crack so that he can hear what it contains; when he hears the news, he carries it to the kitchen for the other servants; the chance to make a good speech or to have the last word in an argument gives Walter full consolation, no matter how serious the disappointment; the latter point is illustrated by the story of the favorite mare and her mule offspring, the former by his extensive, profusely documented oration on death; the word "wife" coming through the open door halts Mrs. Shandy in her tracks; she misunderstands what Walter is saying, and she charges in to accuse him of philandering: "You have one more...than I know of"; he answers with "I have one less [and you don't know about *that*]." And that's why Walter didn't have to mourn his son's death.

(The story of the favorite mare, the Arabian stallion, and the mule has an important echo in the last chapter of *Tristram Shandy* in the story of the Cock and the Bull.)

The events in the kitchen which parallel those in the parlor are part of the human comedy in Tristram Shandy's world. Each of the servants has his own involvement in Bobby's death, each his own selfish (but completely human) response. Death is finally trivial, Tristram seems to suggest; when he presents Trim's oration, the most noteworthy thing he finds to comment on, to draw the reader's attention to, is the eloquence with which Trim dropped his hat to demonstrate how suddenly death strikes. The flirtation between Susannah and Trim—her thinking that the answer to "What is the finest face that ever man looked at" is "Susannah's face"—suffers only a very brief setback when Trim says "corruption"; death affects only the person who dies. There is profundity behind the gay levity of Tristram's storytelling.

The storyteller leaves his mother bent over, listening at the parlor door, as he picks up the thread of parallel events in the kitchen—a digression. But this is more than just an author's trick of presenting simultaneous segments of his story; the implications are uniquely Tristram's: the character is flesh and blood, not just an author's dummy. He has left her for much longer than the scheduled five minutes, and she has a crick in her back from staying bent over. Tristram walks around in the Shandy world; like a stage director, he makes the characters stop and start, but they don't see him (since they're "characters" as well as people). The characters in this world are always vital, but it is a qualified vitality: they are dynamic and they are static — and at the same time. These simultaneous conditions supply one of the basic tensions of the novel, a strange but somehow convincing dualism. The Shandys are allowed their independent movement and direction, but they are always subject to the laws of Tristram's consciousness of them. That consciousness, although it does not interfere with their character and their behavior, provides the sunlight by which we see them or the darkness that hides them from us.

Tristram had promised, among other things, a Chapter on Chambermaids and a Chapter on Buttonholes. He unites the two themes to suggest a bawdy interrelationship, and he offers this as an excuse for not writing about them: no bawdry in *his* book! The "chapter in lieu of it" —Chap. 7—is bawdier, but only because of what he says about it in Chap. 8: it is a "chapter of *chamber-maids, green-gowns, and old hats.*" Without a footnote, however, no one would even notice it.

With Trim's mention of the story of the "poor lieutenant" (Le Fever), the author prepares the reader for something he will take up 40 chapters later (in Bk. 6, Chap. 6). Trim points out the parallel with something that only he knows about, i.e., Toby will "sigh in his bed for a whole month together" about Bobby's death, just as he did when "Le Fever" died. And that is all that Tristram wants to say about the matter here. The author knows what he wants where.

Chapters 15-25

Summary

"Had this volume been a farce," Tristram says, the first 14 chapters would have been the first act. But it isn't a farce, he maintains; by way of transition to the next portion, he speaks of his love of fiddling and his sensitivity to great violin performances.

Walter decides to write a "Tristra-*paedia,* or system of education" for his son. It is his last chance to undo the damage done by the accidents of "geniture, nose, and name." He works at it with the utmost dedication, "with the most painful diligence," and at the end of three years he had "advanced almost into the middle of his work." Since he has begun at the beginning, however, with instructing his son from his birth onward, "the first part of the work, upon which my father had spent the most of his pains, was rendered entirely useless, — every day a page or two became of no consequence." "He advanced so very slow with his work, and I began to live and get forwards at such a rate...." And then something special happened.

"— 'Twas nothing, — I did not lose two drops of blood by it — 'twas not worth calling in a surgeon, had he lived next door to us — thousands suffer by choice, what I did by accident." "The chamber-maid forgot to put a "******* *** [chamber pot] under the bed." Susannah raises little Tristram up to the window seat, lifts the window with one hand, and asks the child if he will, for this once, "**** *** ** *** ******." Down came the window "like lightening upon us; — Nothing is left, — cried *Susannah*, — nothing is left—for me," but to flee the country. But since Uncle Toby's house was closer, she fled there instead. Thus Tristram was circumcised.

When Susannah tells Corporal Trim about the accident, he realizes that it is his fault, and in order to explain that, Tristram must backtrack.

Uncle Toby had told Trim that they needed more cannon for the fortifications. To get lead for the cannon, Trim had been cutting off drain spouts, rain gutters, and other such things. For this particular request—"a couple of field pieces to mount in the gorge of that new redoubt"—Trim took the two lead weights from the nursery window. "He had dismantled every sash window in my uncle *Toby*'s house long before, in the very same way."

Trim could have kept the matter to himself and let Susannah take the blame, but "he determined at once, not to take shelter behind *Susannah*." He marched in with Susannah "to lay the whole *manoeuvre* before" Uncle Toby, who at that moment was giving Parson Yorick "an account of the Battle of *Steenkirk*." Toby at once takes the blame on himself since, as he says to Trim, "You obeyed your orders." A brief discussion of a similar situation involving military obedience follows (the bad behavior of Count Solmes at the battle of Steenkirk), and after the normal amount of military discussion, all four set off for Shandy Hall. En route, Trim says that he wishes he had cut off the church spout instead of taking the sash weights; Yorick answers: "You have cut off spouts enow."

No one could imagine how his father would react to a new situation, says Tristram; "His road lay so very far on one side, from that wherein most men travelled." To explain, Tristram must go back (i.e., to the accident itself; he has already gone past it). Critics must not mind because "provided he keeps along the line of his story," an author "may go backwards and forwards as he will."

Commentary

Apart from the division of the individual volumes of the book into chapters, some "normal" and others mere asides or statements underlining the point of the normal chapters, the author clearly has a plan of organization constantly in mind. The first 14 chapters of Bk. 5. deal with rhetoric on death and with Walter's response to Bobby's death. When that is over with, the author presents the second theme of this volume, his father's scheme for Tristram's education: the Tristra-paedia.

In writing his manual for the education of Tristram, Walter has the same problems that his son will have later in composing his Life and Opinions. To put it another way, Tristram has inherited his father's characteristics; the family resemblance between father and son is obvious. The trouble that Walter has in keeping his instruction abreast of his son's growth is the same thing that Tristram complains of in Bk. 4, Chap. 13: "I am this month one whole year older than I was this time twelve-month; and having got...almost into the middle of my fourth volume — and no farther than to my first day's life — 'tis demonstrative that I have three hundred and sixty-four days more life to write just now, than when I first set out."

The story of the accidental circumcision — not an accident of the same magnitude as the other Accidents — is sprung on us first by Tristram's saying that the consequences of something were trivial and then by showing us the scene itself. The use of asterisks for the indelicate object (the chamber pot) and the indelicate action is itself delicate and interesting: the reader easily succeeds in filling in the words — one letter for each asterisk, with a space between words — and he is pleased with his detective work; then, if he is a Victorian reader, he is offended at the author's coarseness.

Tristram's control of syntax and the pause between phrases is masterfully demonstrated in Susannah's horrorstruck cry: "Nothing is left...." Fortunately, she exaggerates.

To explain the cause of the accident, Tristram must obviously digress and go back to show cause and effect: two more cannon are required for the Toby-Trim minifortifications; lead is required for casting cannon; no more lead remains to be plundered in Toby's house; sash weights are a good source of lead; the nursery windows at Shandy Hall are the last used; Susannah didn't know that when she raised the window it wouldn't stay up. And there we have it. As Tristram suggests, how else could one have told this story? When we consider the alternative of straight-line, natural sequence of time narration (e.g., One day Trim needed more lead for cannon, so he did this and that; and one day shortly afterward, Susannah asked Tristram to urinate out of the window, and then the window fell down), we see that it just wouldn't have been worth it: emphasis, point of view, piquancy would all have been lost. And then, how could Tristram have justified the "One day Trim needed more lead for cannon"?

The comic-epic quality is present in the troop that marches to Shandy Hall. They have discussed problems of military stategy, and a frontal attack is clearly the only maneuver possible. Attack is not necessary, however, since the unpredictable Walter is about to find that the accident is a blessing in disguise. And once again, there is no way that Tristram can present his father's reaction without digressing backward to the scene of the accident.

Chapters 26-43

Summary

The child screams, and his mother comes running to the nursery; Susannah, meanwhile, makes her escape down the back stairs, telling the story in mid-flight to the cook. Walter learns of it from Obadiah. He takes a look and then retires to his library to consult the classical authorities on the value of circumcision. His conclusion is that if all the nations of antiquity, "if SOLON and PYTHAGORAS submitted — what is TRISTRAM? — Who am I, that I should fret or fume one moment about the matter?"

With good humor, Walter tells the advancing party, "This *Tristram* of ours, I find, comes very hardly by all his religious rites. — Never was the son of *Jew, Christian, Turk,* or *Infidel* initiated into them in so oblique and slovenly a manner." As Walter and Yorick bandy back and forth the opinions of the authorities, Toby is unable to figure out his nephew's condition. Apropos of Toby's question of what a "polemic divine" is, Yorick tells the story of Gymnast and Tripet; Toby and Trim do not understand.

Walter decides to read to the assembled a "short chapter or two" of his Tristra-paedia; Toby and Trim settle back to suffer since, as Walter says, "The first thirty pages…are a little dry." The manual for Tristram's education begins with an introduction to "political or civil government" designed to show "the foundation of the natural relation between a father and his child." Quite natural, says Yorick. When Walter quotes Justinian's *The son ought to pay her* [i.e., his mother] *respect*," Yorick says that he can read that in the Catechism. Toby comments: "*Trim* can repeat every word of it by heart." Yorick asks Trim to quote the Fifth Commandment, but Toby points out that it must be asked properly. He raises his voice and gives the command: "The fifth — " "I must begin with the first, an' please your honour, said the corporal." When he finally gets to the fifth, Walter finds an inspired moral: " — SCIENCES MAY BE LEARNED BY ROTE, BUT WISDOM NOT." Walter is sure that Trim has no "idea annexed to any one word he has repeated," but when he asks Trim what he means by honoring his father and mother, Trim gives an answer that pleases Yorick mightily: "Allowing them, an' please your honour, three halfpence a day out of my pay, when they grew old." And since Trim really did so, Walter is bested once again.

Going on to the next chapter, Walter discourses on Health: "The whole secret of health" depends on the struggle for supremacy between "the radical heat and the radical moisture." Yorick asks whether Walter has proved it, and Walter says complacently that he has — and only that. Yorick is spared the proof, but not the reader: Tristram describes his father's proofs and reasoning, how he built his theory on the rubble that he made of Francis Bacon's hypothesis. Walter continues with his interpretation of radical heat and radical moisture ("an oily and balsamous substance") and their importance to the child; his conclusion is simple: "…if a child, as he grows up, can but be taught to avoid running into fire or water, as either of 'em threaten his destruction, — 'twill be all that is needful to be done upon that head."

Meanwhile, a conference has been going on between Toby and Trim. Their interpretation of "radical heat and radical moisture" differs quite a bit from Walter's, and Toby begins the explanation.

Both Toby and Trim were very sick with fever and "flux" at the siege of Limerick. Trim took care of his master and maintained the balance between radical heat and radical moisture "by reinforcing the fever...with hot wine and spices...so that the radical heat stood its ground from the beginning to the end, and was a fair match for the moisture, terrible as it was." Walter is about to blow up with impatience at Toby's theory, but Yorick restrains him and asks Corporal Trim what *his* opinion is on the subject.

The corporal gets into his orator's stance and as he is about to begin, Dr. Slop waddles in. Walter asks about his son as carelessly as if he were inquiring about "the amputation of the tail of a puppy-dog." Dr. Slop is pompous and professional; when he answers, Toby says, "I am no wiser than I was."

Trim begins with a description of the topography of Limerick: "devilish wet, swampy country." Radical moisture "is nothing in the world but ditch-water [i.e., in a soldier's tent] — and...the radical heat, of those who can go to the expence of it, is burnt brandy ['which took off the damp of the air, and made the inside of the tent as warm as a stove']." Dr. Slop doesn't understand what kind of "medical lecture" this is supposed to be, and he speculates that "this poor fellow...has had the misfortune to have heard some superficial emperic discourse upon this nice point." All agree, even Walter.

Dr. Slop returns to his little patient, and Tristram promises that after one more chapter of the Tristra-paedia, the book "shall not be opened again this twelve-month. — Huzza! — "

A person might grow old before learning enough to become truly intelligent — illustrated profusely — and Walter intends to prevent this happening to his son: "I am convinced, *Yorick*,...that there is a North-west passage [i.e., a short cut] to the intellectual world...." Fortunately for little Tristram, he has a parent able "to point it out." The secret: " — The whole entirely depends, added my father, in a low voice, upon the *auxiliary verbs*, Mr. *Yorick*."

Walter explains his theory about auxiliaries (Trim mistakes them for soldiers): "by the right use and application of these" (*"am, was, have, had, do, did,"* etc., etc.), a child can exercise his memory and imagination. After asking Trim whether he has ever seen a white bear (he hasn't), Walter shows how it is possible to talk "intelligently" about one all the same: "A WHITE BEAR! Very well. Have I ever seen one? Might I ever have seen one? Am I ever to see one? Ought I ever to have seen one? Or can I ever see one?" This interesting monologue finally concludes with "Is it better than a BLACK ONE?"

Commentary

The digression explaining the cause of the accident is finished; Susannah's flight to Uncle Toby's house, her reception there, and the parade to Shandy Hall have been described; *then*, finally, the author allows the child to scream. All of this (Chaps. 18-25) is told between the falling of the window and the resulting scream: two kinds of time — remote past (why the window fell) and future subsequent (what Susannah and others did after it fell) — are sandwiched between one instant and the next. By means of this clever device, these events seem simultaneous, but of course they aren't. The author manages to create the effect of simultaneity; we are breathless from so many things happening "instantly." The real events aren't even parallel in time, as we notice immediately: the window falls, the child screams, Susannah flees, etc.

Parallel events, however, are introduced to get the actions back into "real" time:

> Susannah tells Trim; Trim tells his master; the party is formed; they march; they arrive.
> Walter examines his son; he examines his books; he is satisfied; he tells the arriving party his conclusions.

As usual, if classical authorities speak favorably of something, Walter is content to go along with them. This is the unpredictable reaction that Tristram hinted at in Chap. 24. There is always (almost always) wit and humor to be found in Walter, as we see in his comment on the manner of Tristram's circumcision. His son, the author, gets that from him; and although Tristram doesn't have his father's undeviating devotion to "authority," he enjoys erudition if only to laugh at it.

The battle between Gymnast and Tripet — a story taken from Rabelais' *Gargantua and Pantagruel*, Bk. 1, Chap. 35, almost verbatim (Yorick is, after all, reading) — is hard to follow: a "polemic divine" argues and reasons, reasons and argues; his rhetorical and polemical gymnastics resemble the incredible gyrations of Gymnast. Trim's solution — "One home thrust of a bayonet is worth it all" — is actually Rabelais' resolution of the battle: Gymnast skewers Tripet.

As Tristram's book mirrors Tristram, Walter's Tristra-paedia mirrors Walter. The dryness of the erudition is fascinating; Walter writes like his heroes. It is quite often true that, for Walter, the elegant language and the reputation of the writer are more important than the point being made. When he cites Justinian's *Institutes* ("the first book ...at the eleventh title and the tenth section") to support the idea that *"the son ought to pay* [his mother] *respect,"* Yorick counters with the obvious: the same thing may be found much more easily in the Fifth Commandment. That's too folksy for Walter, however, and when Trim recites the Commandments, Walter is sure that it is meaningless to him. Trim's very specific interpretation and his simple human action (giving his aged parents three halfpence a day) make the scholar's pedantry seem empty in contrast.

The following section of the Tristra-paedia, on Health, is full of learning, and it would be a monstrous bore if Tristram had not known what he was doing. Walter comments at length on Hippocrates' and Francis Bacon's *("Lord Verulam")* hypotheses about radical heat and moisture. His high-flown scientific rhetoric falls to earth with the most resounding thud: to keep a child healthy, don't let him drown or burn to death. We can be sure that Tristram has no illusions about the value of his father's erudition.

When Trim gives his interpretation of the significance of radical heat and moisture — military, of course — both Walter and Dr. Slop are disdainful. Yet Trim's view is worth as much as (no more than, but as much as) Walter's scholarship-bedecked conclusion.

Walter's sense of humor can be seen in the exchange between Dr. Slop and Trim. Regarding Trim's explanation, Dr. Slop says he has obviously been listening to "superficial...discourse" on the subject. Walter, who has just been giving a discourse on the subject, says "That he has." (We mustn't exclude the possibility that Walter means something different: Trim has been listening to *someone else* besides Walter.)

The author sympathizes with the reader who has to bear up under the weight of the "learning" quoted from the Tristra-paedia. After promising the reader only one more chapter, he makes the reader say "Hurray!" It is easy to put up with an author who really knows when he is boring the reader, who apologizes for what he "has to" do for the sake of his art.

Walter's chapter on the Auxiliary Verbs is worth about as much as his chapter on Health. His proposed shortcut to intelligence supposedly guarantees control not only of grammar, syntax, and logic, but also of knowledge itself. This contention is "proved" by his "conjugation" of *a white bear*. Tristram is making fun of a theory of education that had been proposed in the preceding century; since Sterne has made Tristram his contemporary and put him in the same environment, Tristram may credibly comment on exactly the same things Sterne would comment on — and still be a character in a novel.

The "intelligent discourse" provided for by this system of "pattern practice" is given perspective by the final sentence in the chapter (and the volume): about this white bear, "Is it better than a BLACK ONE?"

BOOK 6

Chapters 1-13

Summary

Before going on with his story, Tristram looks back at the five volumes already completed. The critics (called "Jack Asses") "view'd and review'd" the earlier volumes, and "good God! what a braying did they all set up together!" Tristram feels that he and his reader ("dear Sir") were lucky to get away with their lives.

Closing his Tristra-paedia, Walter chats with Yorick about famous men who were child prodigies. There were "*Grotius, Scioppius, Heinsius, Politian, Pascal, Joseph Scaliger, Ferdinand de Cordouè,* and others——." Yorick reminds him of the "great *Lipsius,*...who composed a work the day he was born." Uncle Toby, always literal-minded, remarks: "They should have wiped it up,...and said no more about it."

Back in the nursery, Dr. Slop and Susannah are arguing: she is bashful about holding the candle as the doctor works on the child, and he accuses her of false modesty and of worse things. Holding the candle with her eyes averted, Susannah accidentally sets fire to Dr. Slop's wig. Recriminations and name-calling follow, and they douse each other with the basinful of "cataplasm" intended for Tristram's cure. Then, since that treatment had failed, they "retired into the kitchen to prepare a fomentation" for him.

Walter thinks that it is time to get Tristram a tutor: "You see 'tis high time, said my father, addressing himself equally to my uncle *Toby* and *Yorick*, to take this young creature out of these women's hands, and put him into those of a private governor." He outlines the many necessary good qualities of the ideal tutor, and Uncle Toby asks him to give the post to "poor *Le Fever*'s son." Tristram regrets having lost the opportunity earlier of having Trim tell the story of Le Fever: "—fool that I was! nor can I recollect, (nor perhaps you) without turning back to the place, what it was that hindered me from letting the corporal tell it in his own words; —but the occasion is lost, —I must tell it now in my own."

The Story of LE FEVER

In 1706 — "in the summer of that year in which *Dendermond* was taken by the allies" — Uncle Toby was having his supper one evening, Trim respectfully waiting on him. The landlord of a small inn came to the house to request "a glass or two of sack" for a sick army officer lying at his inn; the officer has with him his son, "a boy...of about eleven or twelve years of age." Toby naturally gives the landlord several bottles of the wine, and afterward he sends Trim to learn what he can of the affair. While he is waiting, Toby "might be said to have thought of nothing else but poor *Le Fever* and his boy" — "had it not been, that he now and then wandered from the point, with considering whether it was not full as well to have the curtain of the tennaile a straight line, as a crooked one."

Trim comes back to report. The soldier, already ill, had arrived without a servant, and the landlady is sure that he will die. In the kitchen, Trim made friends with the young son after identifying himself as an old soldier, and he was taken up to Le Fever's room. It turns out that "Captain Toby Shandy" is known by name to the sick soldier, and Le Fever — whose wife "was most unfortunately killed with a musket shot" — is known by that circumstance to Uncle Toby. Toby is so moved by the situation of the sick father, the dead wife, and the devoted son that he says, "I wish, *Trim*, I was asleep."

"To my uncle *Toby*'s eternal honour," in spite of his being "warmly engaged at that time in carrying on the siege of *Dendermond*, parallel with the allies" — i.e., in the minifortifications — he gave it up and devoted his attention completely to Le Fever. He makes plans for calling in the best available doctor, moving Le Fever and his son to his own house, and his and Trim's nursing the lieutenant. Trim, however, is pessimistic about the future: "In a fortnight or three weeks, added my uncle *Toby*, smiling, —he might march. —He will never march, an' please your honour, in this world, said the corporal.... he will never march, but to his grave." They debate the point, Trim hopeless, Toby hopeful. "The poor soul will die: —He shall not die, by G—, cried my uncle *Toby.*" And immediately, " — The ACCUSING SPIRIT which flew up to heaven's chancery with the oath, blush'd as he gave it in, — and the RECORDING ANGEL as he wrote it down, dropp'd a tear upon the word, and blotted it out for ever."

Toby orders Trim to "go early in the morning for a physician," then goes to bed.

The next morning Toby visits Le Fever, who is at the point of death; although the lieutenant is unable to respond vocally to Toby's frank generosity and goodness, he is aware of them. His son also recognizes Toby's kind, fatherly nature. The author describes Le Fever's dying moments with a certain amount of impatience: "...the pulse fluttered — stopp'd — went on — throb'd — stopp'd again — moved — stopp'd — shall I go on? — No."

Having killed off Le Fever, the author plans to tell the rest of the story "in a very few words" ("I am so impatient to return to my own story..."). First, however, he tells of Yorick's funeral sermon for Le Fever, and then of the interesting marginal notes that he has found on the manuscripts of Yorick's sermons; he learns a lot (and so do we) about Yorick from them, and he speculates about Yorick's methods of composition, his confessions, and his attitudes toward his sermons.

Uncle Toby administers Le Fever's "estate" — "an old regimental coat and a sword." The former he gives to Trim ("Wear it, *Trim,* said my uncle *Toby,* as long as it will hold together, for the sake of the poor lieutenant..."); the latter he puts aside for young Billy, whom he has virtually adopted. He sees to the boy's schooling, and he treats him like a son.

In the "spring of the year, seventeen" — Billy is then about 22 years old — the young man is fired by "the stories of the emperor's sending his army into *Hungary* against the *Turks....*" He leaves school and begs Uncle Toby to let him go off to war. In possession of his father's old sword, the blessing of Uncle Toby, and a purse of sixty guineas (from Toby), he sets off to seek his fortune in war. Misfortune and sickness, however, are all he finds, and he decides to return to the welcoming bosom of his foster father.

He is "hourly expected...and...uppermost in my uncle *Toby*'s mind" as Walter describes the ideal tutor for Tristram. Although Toby begs Walter to consider young Le Fever for the post, Walter is annoyed by certain related military small talk; thinking perhaps that *three* military men in one household would be too many, he puts the matter off, and that's the end of it.

Commentary

In the periodic review that Tristram makes of his production up to a given point, he talks about critics and their reviews of the previous installment. Sterne gives Tristram the prerogative of making these comments because, after all, Tristram Shandy is supposed to be writing the *Life and Opinions of Tristram Shandy.* The character has been created, the book he writes is real, critics actually review this book, and the character—improbable or not—reviews the reviewers.

Things are still going wrong for little Tristram: he can't even get adequate medical attention. The fight between Susannah and Dr. Slop delays the treatment, and although the burning of Slop's wig is hilariously comic, we must remember that "the sport of small accidents, *Tristram Shandy"* is waiting for his wound to be bound up. Dr. Slop's rumor-mongering—to be presented shortly—probably got its impetus from the rough handling he received from Susannah.

The matter of hiring a tutor for little Tristram leads the author to Le Fever, father and son. When we look at the framework of main story and Le Fever story, we see Tristram's skill in plotting: the child needs a tutor, Toby recommends "young Le Fever," we need an explanation of who Le Fever is. The author's professional attitude toward his book is again seen: are his characters simply characters, or are they real people? Tristram pretends that he doesn't remember where he first brought up the name of Le Fever (it was in Bk. 5, Chap. 10), and then he regrets not having had Trim tell the story then and there—as if it would have been less work for the author! As it is, however, Tristram must now tell it in his own words.

It should be obvious to us that this is the point where the story belongs; had he allowed Trim to tell it back there, it would have delayed the "action," and it would have been an indefensible digression.

The story of Le Fever is an exercise in goodheartedness and sentimentalism. Through the magnanimous and generous response of Uncle Toby to the poor, forlorn lieutenant and his son, the sentimental reader is able to renew his faith in Human Nature. Toby's philanthropy, his compassion for the Le Fevers, is moving and convincing, and there is no doubt that the author partakes, together with the reader, of the sense of euphoric goodness and well-being stimulated by Toby's actions. Still, there are two sides to Tristram's personality: the traditional and the countertraditional. Everyone without exception will be delighted by the little fairy tale that follow's Toby's oath—his only oath in the book: "He shall not die, by G—." The "ACCUSING SPIRIT" reluctantly does his duty and carries the message up to the accounting department; the "RECORDING ANGEL"—like a good, generous, eighteenth-century clerk —also doing his duty, writes it down in Toby's debit column, and then juggles the books by blotting out the entry with a well-placed teardrop. It is a delicious little story, and even the most self-righteous nineteenth-century reader may have shed a companion tear and similarly have forgiven Toby.

Everyone can be counted a pushover for that scene, but not everyone could forgive the author for toying around with Le Fever's death scene: his pulse stopped, started, stopped, started—until the author is frankly tired of it. If we're not sure, he puts us out of doubt: "I am so impatient to return to my own story...." The author likes a neat bit of sentiment—sometimes a sizable chunk—because it's good for people. But he also feels the inherent ridiculousness of using sentiment for a tonic; he therefore undoes what he did. There are even a few little clues that good old Toby himself may be somewhat more selfishly human than one suspects: he "thought of nothing else but poor *Le Fever* and his boy" except that "he now and then wandered from the point," thinking of whether a straight line or a crooked line was better for a part of the fortifications. (We might, if we wish, choose an obvious alternative: it was impossible for Toby to think of anything in the world without being distracted sooner or later by military matters.)

The "marginal notes" in Yorick's sermons remind us a good deal of Tristram's commentary on his own writing—except for the obvious fact that Yorick is a parson and Tristram is a novelist; that difference, however, is sufficient to keep the two individuals separate, as they should be. Yorick, as a companion of Walter Shandy, was a formative influence in Tristram's life; if they remind us of each other occasionally, the novel gives us good reason for that. We can and we ought to forget that Sterne was both a parson and a novelist: that biographical datum leads us only to a series of non-fruitful "revelations" like "Yorick is Sterne," "Tristram is Sterne," "Yorrick *and* Tristram are Sterne," etc.

The sufficient reason for Tristram's going into the matter of Yorick's sermons is the funeral sermon of Le Fever; the sufficient reason for going into the Le Fever history is Toby's being able to propose the son — old enough by now — as Tristram's tutor. Everything fits.

Chapters 14-19

Summary

Dr. Slop, "like a son of a w——, as my father called him," spreads a rumor that the accident with the window had disastrous results, *"that poor Master Shandy * * * * * * * * * * * * * * * en-*tirely"; and even worse than that, "that the nursery window had not only * * * * *...; — but that * * * * *...also." Walter is furi-ous, and Toby recommends putting the child on display "at the market cross."

Walter decides to dress the child in breeches (i.e., tight pants), but he reached this decision only after prolonged discussion with Mrs. Shandy in what he calls his "beds of justice."

The "beds of justice" were Walter's equivalent of a "wise custom" of the "ancient *Goths* of *Germany*," that "of debating every thing of importance to their state, twice...once drunk, and once sober." Walter, who was "entirely a water-drinker," finally found a way to approximate that "wise custom": "he fixed and set apart the first *Sunday* night in the month, and the *Saturday* night which immediately preceded it, to argue it over, in bed with my mother." (The reader will remember that the novel begins on the first Sunday night of a month — March, 1718.)

Tristram takes us to the scene of the discussion:

> We should begin, said my father, turning himself half round in bed, and shifting his pillow a little towards my mother's, as he opened the debate —— We should begin to think, Mrs. *Shandy*, of putting this boy into breeches. ——
> We should so, —— said my mother. —— We defer it, my dear, quoth my father, shamefully. ——
> I think we do, Mr. *Shandy*, —— said my mother.

The "discussion" goes on, Mr. Shandy trying to get Mrs. Shandy to do more than simply agree; she never does more, however. Walter gives up; "this was on the *Sunday* night," Tristram says waggishly.

Walter searches the texts of the Authorities for advice about breeches, but although the wardrobe of the ancients is described in fine detail, he can find no word about breeches. By devious and arbitrary reasoning—"My father lost the horse, but not the saddle"—he manages to conclude that Tristram's breeches should be made "with hooks and eyes."

Commentary

Using asterisks rather more broadly—we can't work out the specific words this time—the author manages to convey approximately what people are saying about Tristram's accident; there is no doubt in anyone's mind that the window did a thorough job. It is all an exaggeration, however. Toby, as usual, recommends the direct route: show the child (naked, we assume) in public. Walter, devious as ever, decides that breeches will serve to outline little Tristram's manly build.

Always trying to model his life and actions along the lines laid out by the ancients, Walter uses his quaint domestic arrangements to help him arrive at a considered judgment. The bedroom scene is as funny for the picture it gives us of Mrs. Shandy's "reasoning" as it is for itself: Mrs. Shandy cannot argue, discuss, or question. There is no way that Walter can provoke her into his kind of intellectual activity or, for that matter, into any kind of intellectual activity. She is content.

Even for a decision about what kind of breeches to get for the child, Walter must consult scholarly books. Although he doesn't find anything on breeches, he comes up with information (mistaken) about how to fasten them.

Chapters 20-32

Summary

Tristram announces a "new scene of events." He is going to leave everything: "the breeches in the taylor's hands," "my mother," "*Slop* ...[with] the full profits of all my dishonours," "*Le Fever* to recover, and get home from *Marseilles*" as best he can. He would even leave himself, "but 'tis impossible,—I must go along with you to the end of the work."

He takes us back to the beginnings of Toby and Trim's fortifications, showing us what they built and how they went about it. The soil was good, the plans were precise, and Toby and Trim enjoyed it all. They would stake out in exact proportion the town currently under siege; then Trim would dig the ditches and build parapets and towers to scale. As the battle progressed, they moved accordingly: Toby, "with the *Gazette* in his hand," Trim "with a spade on his shoulder to execute the contents." They destroyed according to the newspaper description, also in exact proportion: "What intense pleasure swimming in his eye as he stood over the corporal, reading the paragraph ten times over to him, as he was at work, lest, peradventure, he should make the breach an inch too wide, — or leave it an inch too narrow."

They continued "in this track of happiness for many years," since it was a long war. Instead of a new suit for Christmas one year, Toby "treated himself with a handsome sentry-box" ("in case of rain"). After that, they had "a little model of a town built for them," and this town served for *all* the towns successively under siege: "It was *Landen,* and *Trerebach,* and *Santvliet,* and *Drusen,* and *Hagenau,* — and then it was *Ostend* and *Menin,* and *Aeth* and *Dendermond.*" The only thing missing was ammunition for the little "brass field pieces." It was just as well, says Tristram: "For so full were the papers...of the incessant firings kept up by the besiegers, — and so heated was my uncle *Toby's* imagination with the accounts of them, that he...[would have] infallibly shot away all his estate." Trim supplied a solution, and "this will not be explained the worse, for setting off, as I generally do, at a little distance from the subject."

Trim's unfortunate brother, Tom (his misfortunes are spoken of in Bk. 2, Chap. 17, and Bk. 4, Chap. 4), had sent him "a *Montero*-cap and two *Turkish* tobacco pipes," and Trim has a plan. Before describing Trim's plan, Tristram eulogizes him — "Tread lightly on his ashes, ye men of genius, — for he was your kinsman" — and wishes that he were alive to share the benefits of Tristram's prosperity. He also looks to the future when, in his book, he must tell about the death of Uncle Toby: "Gracious powers!...when I shall arrive at this dreaded page, deal not with me, then, with a stinted hand."

Trim hooks up the tubes of the long Turkish tobacco pipes to the base of the cannon, loads them with tobacco, and begins to "fire" them. He is puffing away furiously when Toby arrives for the day's battle. "'Twas well for my father," comments Tristram, "that my uncle *Toby* had not his will to make that day." Toby is enchanted: "My uncle *Toby* smiled, — then looked grave, — then smiled for a moment, — then looked serious for a long time; — Give me hold of the ivory pipe, Trim...."

Tristram asks the reader's help in wheeling off the cannon and the rest of the fortifications behind the scene, so that he can "exhibit my uncle *Toby* dressed in a new character." The reason that the "greatest heroes of ancient and modern story" "never felt what the sting of love was" is simple: "...they had all of them something else to do." Toby was among them until "Fate...basely patched up the peace of *Utrecht.*"

The Treaty of Utrecht was a great blow to Toby, and Walter naturally thinks that Toby is merely disappointed about the "loss of his *hobby-horse.*" He consoles him: "Never mind, brother *Toby,*...by God's blessing we shall have another war break out again some of these days." Toby defends himself from the implication that he is a warmonger, and although he was not usually an eloquent person, he waxes eloquent on this subject. Tristram found a speech of Toby's among his father's papers: Walter was "so highly pleased with one of these apologetical orations of my uncle *Toby's,* which he had delivered one evening before him and *Yorick,* that he wrote it down before he went to bed."

Toby is aware that when a man wishes for war, "it has an ill aspect to the world." But he asks Walter whether he really thinks that in condemning the peace of Utrecht, Toby wants "more of his fellow creatures slain, — more slaves made, and more families driven from their peaceful habitations, merely for his own pleasure." He hates the cruelty of war as much as anyone, but man is forced into it "by NECESSITY." English wars have been fought "upon principles of *liberty,* and upon principles of *honour*"; their wars have been "the getting together of quiet and harmless people, with their swords in their hands, to keep the ambitious and the turbulent within bounds." The pleasure that Toby and Trim get from their fortifications and war games comes from their consciousness that they "were answering the great ends of our creation."

Commentary

The new scene of events features Toby as chief actor — at least until the end of Bk. 6. The previous story and its consequences — Tristram's last accident — are dropped: Tristram is leaving everyone behind, including himself (that is, little Tristram and his misfortunes); as storyteller, however, he must obviously go along with us to the end of the work even though he has no part in these new events.

The genesis of Toby's fortifications is shown us in detail; earlier we were told only that they went and engaged in the activity. Now we see just how they conducted their sieges parallel with those reported in the newspapers, and we can understand just how satisfying their involvement was to them. All of their ingenuity comes forward as they solve one problem after another in constructing their models and equivalent situations. The solution that Trim comes up with to make the cannon smoke is an admirable one, and Toby's joy is a delight to us. Tristram's presentation of Trim's solution is the familiar one of backing away and then coming up to the point, including the necessary background as he returns: Trim had once received from his brother a present of souvenirs, the cap and the Turkish pipes.

The author in his dual role of deliberate craftsman and participant in the lives of the other characters once more emerges: he knows that he will have to (at least he says that he intends to) describe at some future time the death of Uncle Toby, in writing his complete Life and Opinions, and he hopes for the necessary competence; he tells how he and his father felt at the funeral of their beloved uncle and brother. This dear Uncle Toby character is so real that we also can mourn his death — even if it doesn't occur in the book (except at this "timeless" point).

Although Tristram hasn't managed to change the scene radically, he is trying to: first he focuses exclusively on Toby, and then he will somehow make him fall in love. His explanation of why Toby never fell in love is adequate: besides his modesty — a *very* important characteristic, as we will see near the end of the story — he has been wrapped up in his military maneuvers. Wearing his stage-director hat, Tristram reminds us of the dimensions within his story: *we* are to help him move around the scenery, wheel away the cannon and the sentry box. We aren't readers of a mere novel; we aren't even passive spectators at a play. We are participants in Tristram's theater, and if we don't help him, maybe the show couldn't go on.

Having established his presence by now, Tristram doesn't really need to give explanations about the source of his information, how he learned, for example, about Toby's "apologetical oration." Toby made his speech five years before Tristram's birth, after all. Nevertheless, the author keeps us happy by avoiding the anachronism: Walter had written it down, and Tristram found it. One can't object to this as a farfetched "gimmick," even if he felt like it, because the author is wise enough to include Walter's marginal comments and even to raise his eyebrows at the comments.

Toby's oration is both convincing and unconvincing. As a rationalization about the necessity for war, it would probably pass muster;

nobody could after all imagine that Toby would delight in war for the sake of glory, thrills, and excitement. And yet, after Toby had made it plain that war is sometimes a bitter but necessary duty, there is overwhelming bathos in the juxtaposition of "that infinite delight...[from] my sieges in my bowling green" and "the consciousness...that in carrying them [i.e., the sieges] on, we were answering the great ends of our creation." Although Toby is innocent, Tristram must surely see the ridiculousness of his statement; his love for his uncle, however, keeps him from commenting, we may assume. At any rate, Walter doesn't seem to be convinced by Toby's "oration," and he doesn't hesitate to say so.

Chapters 33-40

Summary

Tristram reiterates the principle behind his storytelling: "...when a man is telling a story in the strange way I do mine, he is obliged continually to be going backwards and forwards to keep all tight together in the reader's fancy." He tries to keep the reader from getting lost; then he gets lost himself! "But 'tis my father's fault," as the reader will see when Tristram's "brains come to be dissected." He decides to begin the chapter over again.

Uncle Toby did not "dismount his [hobby] horse at all — his horse rather flung him." During the peace of Utrecht he had nothing to do; then, according to the articles of the treaty, it was stipulated that Dunkirk was to be demolished. He and Trim discuss the best way of destroying their fortifications, and they are once again caught up in the spirit: "...we retreat towards the town; — then we'll demolish the mole, — next fill up the harbour, — then retire into the citadel, and blow it up into the air; and having done that, corporal, we'll embark for *England.* — We are there, quoth the corporal, recollecting himself — Very true, said my uncle *Toby* — looking at the church."

No more war games to play, Toby becomes listless. "The trumpet of war fell out of his hands, — he took up the lute, sweet instrument!" And now it is time, says Tristram, to fulfill his promise to tell about Uncle Toby's courtship of Widow Wadman. He is most confident that it will turn out to be "one of the most compleat systems, both of the elementary and practical part of love and love-making, that ever was addressed to the world." He cites authorities on "love" and learned medical treatises on the physiology of love, and he tells what Walter did to "protect"

Toby from adverse consequences of being in love (one thing Walter did was to have the tailor sew a "camphorated cere-cloth" into Toby's new breeches, as a lining).

Tristram doesn't feel *"obliged* to set out with a definition of what love is." Whatever it is, "my uncle *Toby* fell into it." Widow Wadman is worth falling in love with, Tristram says, " — And possibly, gentle reader, with such a temptation — so wouldst thou." What does she look like? Leaving a page blank in the chapter, Tristram invites the reader to paint his own picture of her, "as like your mistress as you can — as unlike your wife as your conscience will let you — 'tis all one to me — please but your own fancy in it." When that is done, Tristram exclaims, "Was ever any thing in Nature so sweet! — so exquisite!" and he asks, "Then, dear Sir, how could my uncle *Toby* resist it?"

Word gets around between the servants (Susannah and Bridget) that Uncle Toby is in love with Widow Wadman — "fifteen days before it happened." Mrs. Shandy hears of it and tells her husband: "My brother *Toby,* quoth she, is going to be married to Mrs. *Wadman.*" Walter's reply is, "Then he will never...be able to lie *diagonally* in his bed again as long as he lives." And when Mrs. Shandy does not ask him what he means, Walter again grumbles to himself about his sad fate: "That she is not a woman of science...is her misfortune — but she might ask a question." Tristram goes on in his father's vein: "My mother never did. — In short, she went out of the world at last without knowing whether it turned *round,* or stood *still.* — My father had officiously told her above a thousand times which way it was, — but she always forgot."

In the final chapter of this book, Tristram draws diagrams — very irregular ones — to show how the story has progressed through each of the first five books; the sixth one (he says) is much, much straighter, "for from the end of *Le Fever*'s episode, to the beginning of my uncle *Toby*'s campaigns, — I have scarce stepped a yard out of my way." He hopes ("it is not impossible") that the further books of the story will follow an absolutely straight line.

Commentary

There is a funny object-lesson at the beginning of this section: in explaining how he takes pains to keep the reader from getting lost, Tristram loses himself in his explanation. He is demonstrating two facts: 1) it *is* necessary to digress and tamper with natural sequence to tell his kind of story and 2) unless both Tristram and the reader concentrate, one or the other of them will get lost in the novel. We notice also that Tristram reiterates his relationship to Walter Shandy: if something is wrong with his brains, it's his father's fault. Tristram is a Shandy, not a Sterne.

The end of the war is a sad thing for both Toby and Trim. There is poignancy side by side with the basic ridiculousness in their planning the retreat from Dunkirk: they had forgotten they were in England.

The fulfillment of Tristram's promise of the account of Uncle Toby's amours is at hand — but then again, it isn't. In Bk. 4, Chap. 32, we were promised this "choicest morsel of my whole story"; in Bk. 3, Chap. 24, we were told that "a most minute account of every particular ...shall be given in its proper place"; in Bk. 2, Chap. 7, it was hinted at provocatively. But we still don't have it, and we won't get it for quite a while yet. How important can it be, we should ask ourselves. Here, Tristram assures us that it will be one of the best "systems" ever written about. "It had better be good" is all that the reader can say (with patience and resignation).

Audience participation is again elicited by Tristram, and for a most useful purpose. How beautiful and tempting is Widow Wadman? — as beautiful and tempting as *you* want to make her. And if she is that attractive, obviously Uncle Toby couldn't resist her. So he doesn't.

The blank on which we can draw our beautiful Widow Wadman is safe from the critics at whose hands Tristram considers himself illused; they will find nothing to be malicious about here. Incidentally, this is the third of the three "trick" pages that Tristram uses in his book: one was black, one was marbled (half black, half white), one is white.

Mrs. Shandy's nature is again dissected, poor woman. Both father and son have the same opinion of her, although Tristram is more tolerant of her than was his father.

The wild lines with loops, branches, and switchbacks do very nicely as graphs of the "progress" of the several books. It would be understatement to say that Tristram knows as well as we do about how the story has been going. He knows where he is heading, what the reader thinks about the journey, what the reader doesn't know, and how to keep the reader pacified.

BOOK 7

Chapters 1-28

Summary

The author refers to his promise (made in Bk. 1, Chap. 22) to "write two volumes every year" for 40 years – provided that he stays alive and well. But he is not so well; the main thing that buoys him up is his "spirits": "...in no one moment of my existence,...have ye once deserted me,...and when DEATH himself knocked at my door—ye bad him come again; and in so gay a tone of careless indifference, did ye do it, that he doubted of his commission." (He is even miffed by the fact that Death called on him while he was telling a dirty story to Eugenius.)

He decides to flee Death by taking a trip to France, and he describes his travels while he is about it.

The trip across the Channel is quite rough, and he and the other passengers are glad to get ashore. He must then make a choice among the three roads that go from Calais to Paris. Since he is in Calais, he asks himself whether he ought not to describe it. He really doesn't want to, however, and he asks the reader why "a man cannot go quietly through a town, and let it alone, when it does not meddle with him."

He writes a little travelogue description of Calais, nevertheless, gaily offering to add a little history in *"Rapin's* own words" that "will not take up above fifty pages." Kindness keeps him from it: "But courage! gentle reader!— I scorn it— 'tis enough to have thee in my power." Then on to Boulogne.

Feeling himself pursued by Death, Tristram urges the coachman to make haste. His fellow passengers assume that he is pursued by the law, and they speculate in low voices about his crimes. (Tristram, meanwhile, is occupied with flirting with a pretty girl.) He realizes that his desire for haste makes him unfair to the coaches and coachmen, but he can't resist pointing out *that something is always wrong in a French post-chaise upon first setting out"*: "a rope's broke!— a knot has slipt! —a staple's drawn" or the coachman has to get down and take his sandwich out of the bag. A little bribe will usually make him rush, and the coach reaches Montreuil.

The most interesting thing in Montreuil is Janatone, the innkeeper's daughter; she knits and subtly flirts with Tristram, and he is aware of her many charms. The reader would prefer the measurements of the "length, breadth, and perpendicular height of the great parish church, or a drawing of the façade of the abbey of Saint *Austreberte*," Tristram supposes, "but he who measures thee, *Janatone*, must do it now — thou carriest the principles of change within thy frame."

They set off for Abbeville, where the inn makes a bad impression on Tristram. If he could make conditions with Death about where he is to die, he would stipulate that it be "in some decent inn." "But mark. This inn, should not be the inn at *Abbeville* — if there was not another inn in the universe, I would strike that inn out of the capitulation."

Still in a rush to get to Paris, he has a pleasant revery about heathen gods and goddesses at play; he comes to himself with a start: "What jovial times! — but where am I? and into what a delicious riot of things am I rushing? I — I who must be cut short in the midst of my days, and taste no more of 'em than what I borrow from my imagination."

They reach Amiens, about which Tristram has one fact to tell us: "*Janatone* went there to school."

The most irritating thing of the entire trip is having to wake up every six miles to pay his fare, the horses being changed that regularly. He thinks of ways to outwit the collectors, like having the money ready in his hand, but there is always an argument or discussion to go through about some detail or other, or "then Monsieur *le Curé* offers you a pinch of snuff — or a poor soldier shews you his leg — or a shaveling [i.e., begging friar] his box...." Try to get back to sleep after that!

They enter Paris, which "looks, I suppose, better than it smells," and Tristram remarks on the narrowness of the streets, the number of restaurants, and the number of barbershops: "One would think that all the cooks in the world on some great merry-meeting with the barbers, by joint consent had said — Come, let us all go live at *Paris*."

His view of Paris is somewhat soured by his not being able to get a room: "...in all the five hundred grand Hôtels, which they number up to you in *Paris*...the devil a one of us out of fifty, can get our heads fairly thrust in amongst them." He enumerates the 900 streets of Paris, and he quotes the inscription over the Louvre, commenting wryly: "The *French* have a *gay* way of treating every thing that is Great; and that is all can be said upon it."

He rushes on, and he "cannot stop a moment to give you the character of the people — their genius — their manners — their customs — their laws — their religion — their government — their manufactures — their commerce — their finances" (although he is qualified to do so, having spent "three days and two nights amongst them").

Suddenly he turns to understanding the speed – or lack of it – of the coaches in France: "...if you weigh their vehicles with the mountains of baggage which you lay both before and behind upon them — and then consider their puny horses, with the very little they give them — 'tis a wonder they get on at all." Instead of feeding their horses, the French drive them on with two words: "****** and ****** in which there is as much sustenance, as...[in] a peck of corn." He hesitates to use these words himself, but he will illustrate his point with the story of the Abbess of Andoüillets and her novice.

This abbess, suffering from a stiff knee, decides to go to the hot baths at Bourbon; for company she takes a young novice, Margarita, who is suffering with an infected finger. They set out in a carriage driven by the convent gardener, who walks alongside and drinks slyly from his wine bottle. When his wine is finished, the young man gives the mules "a sound lash, and looking in the abbess's and *Margarita*'s faces (as he did it) — as much as to say, 'here I am' — he gave a second good crack — as much as to say to his mules, 'get on' — so slinking behind, he enter'd the little inn at the foot of the hill." The mules get halfway up the hill, and realizing that the driver is no longer there, they stop. The nuns cannot get them to move on, and they feel panic: "We are ruin'd and undone, my child, said the abbess to *Margarita* — we shall be here all night — we shall be plunder'd — we shall be ravish'd — " " — We shall be ravish'd, said *Margarita*, as sure as a gun."

The young nun tells the abbess that there are "two certain words, which I have been told will force any horse, or ass, or mule, to go up a hill whether he will or no." She forces herself to whisper the words. They decide that the sin of saying the words can be avoided if each says only one syllable:

Abbess, ⎫ Margarita, ⎭	Bou - - bou - - bou - - — ger, - - ger, - - ger
Margarita, ⎫ Abbess, ⎭	Fou - - fou - - fou - - — ter, - - ter, - - ter.

The mules do not move. "They do not understand us, cried *Margarita* — But the Devil does, said the abbess of *Andoüillets*."

Tristram admits to "Madam," his reader, that he has been wearing his fool's cap during the last piece of storytelling, and he continues the account of his travels. Apropos of his passing through the town of Auxerre, he remembers that when he was a boy, he and his father, Uncle Toby, Obadiah, and Trim stopped there on a tour of France. Walter was anxious to see the mummies at the Abbey of Saint Germain; he makes an assortment of ribald comments and innuendoes about the proximity of the male saints to the female saints. Toby and Trim of course "mount the ramparts" of the castle to study its fortifications.

The author marvels at the parallel journeys and the repetition of history. His situation astounds him: "I have brought myself into such a situation, as no traveller ever stood before me; for I am this moment walking across the market-place of *Auxerre* with my father and my uncle *Toby,* in our way back to dinner — and I am this moment also entering *Lyons* with my post-chaise broke into a thousand pieces — and I am moreover this moment...[in Toulouse] where I now sit rhapsodizing all these affairs."

Commentary

Book 7, containing the account of Tristram's journey through France (for his health), seems to be isolated from the story that preceded and from the story that follows. Toby's amours will not be told about in this book, after all. Still, within the context of the whole — the life and opinions of Tristram Shandy — this section has as much validity as any other, even if the Shandys are left behind. In addition to the promise of Uncle Toby's famous "amours," the author reminds us that he has promised "two volumes every year," but he hasn't specified the subject of those volumes. The epigraph to Bk. 7 (each of the five installments has one) says, in translation, "For this is not an excursion from it, but is the work itself." The work ultimately is the life and opinions of the "I" of the book.

Tristram's cavalier attitude toward death is consistent with his attitude toward grave matters in general; he is not frightened, impressed, or subued. He treats death like an annoying old bore, someone to get away from. Tristram, like his creator, Laurence Sterne, is consumptive; Sterne had the same gay indifference toward death that he gave to his chief character. This is not to say that they had no concern about whether they lived or died.

The "travelogue" material of Bk. 7 is sprightly and funny. Tristram makes no attempt to sound like a guidebook — except when he makes fun of guidebooks—and yet we learn a lot about France, about the human element in the French and their impact on this funny Englishman. As he says, why can't a traveler go quietly through a town and let it alone instead of writing descriptions about it. In his observations about how something is always wrong with French coaches, about the smell of Paris, the difficulty in finding a hotel room, the number of cooks and barbers, about trying to get some sleep while traveling, about the overloaded coaches and the overworked horses—in all of these we see a real-life France. Spleen and amused tolerance struggle for mastery, but Tristram finally relinquishes the former.

Even though he is pursued by death, Tristram is able to enjoy the beauty of life; he is distracted by the pretty passerby, by the charming Janatone at Montreuil, and (at the end of the book) by the country girl, Nannette. At the same time, the book contains bittersweet (not bitter) references to beauty and happiness cut short by death, as in the apostrophe to Janatone, who carries "the principles of change" in her, and in his own sober realization that he is dying and "must be cut short in the midst of" his days.

Careful planning can again be seen in the introducing of the story of the Abbess of Andoüillets: coach travel is a hard matter; French coaches are very slow; the fault doesn't lie with the horses, however, since they are overburdened; the horses are also underfed; the coachmen get them to move on by means of the two words "****** and ******" (bouger and fouter); he is too much a gentleman to write these words, but he knows a story in which these two words are said and yet not said (since two people each say one syllable).

In Chap. 27 whom do we meet but all the Shandys except Mrs. Shandy. They suddenly pop up in full character and costume: Walter, the satirical pedagogue, guidebook in hand; Toby, as compassionate and military as ever. We might as well be back in Shandy Hall, when Tristram was still a child. But we aren't: we're on a trip with the mature, aging author who has taken time out from his writing about his family and his past to tell about the sudden trip he had to take for his health. We are looking at *three* Tristrams, and the author of course knows it; even he is somewhat awed by the fact. Tristram 1 is the child on the tour with his father and his uncle; Tristram 2 is the subject of Bk. 7, the sick man who is touring France (at the moment he is between Auxerre and Lyons in a wrecked coach); Tristram 3 is the man with the pen in his hand, sitting in Toulouse and writing about what happened to him in Auxerre. Ordinarily, we wouldn't think about the second and third as different individuals; after all, lots of writers write about themselves. There is this difference, however, and it is a difference that Tristram constantly emphasizes: when he himself is the subject of his writing, he discusses the handling of that subject as if it were any other; he puts distance between himself as author and himself as subject (both child and adult).

This chapter shows the author's achievement and success in relation to his intention: "In a word, my work is digressive, and it is progressive too, — and at the same time" (Bk. 1, Chap. 22).

Chapters 29-43

Summary

As he said at the end of the previous chapter, Tristram has coach trouble before he gets to Lyons. He sells the wreck, thinking, as he collects the money, about his ability to salvage something out of every disaster (including a sexual one involving his "dear *Jenny*").

In Lyons he intends to see the "great clock of *Lippius* of *Basil*," "the thirty volumes of the general history of *China*, [written]...in the *Chinese* character," "the house where *Pontius Pilate* lived," and the tomb of the two unfortunate lovers, Amandus and Amanda. (First, he learns that the putative house of Pontius Pilate is in the next town, not in Lyons.) The story of the unfortunate lovers, separated for most of their lives, appeals strongly to him: when they were finally reunited, "they fly into each others arms, and both drop down dead for joy."

On his way to the sights, he is stopped by an ass eating "turnip tops and cabbage-leaves," which is blocking the gate. *"Honesty,"* as he calls the ass, is eating a bitter artichoke stem, and Tristram is moved to feed him a cookie: "Thou hast not a friend perhaps in all this world that will give thee a macaroon." Lest the reader think him sentimental, Tristram confesses that there was more of interest in "seeing *how* an ass would eat a macaroon — than of benevolence in giving him one...." Someone beats the ass and drives it away, and Tristram's breeches are torn by a ragged edge of the pannier.

His trousers fixed, he sets out again; at the same spot he meets the person who had driven off the ass. It is a "commissary" who has come to collect "some six livres odd sous" that Tristram supposedly owes for the coach trips he has canceled. Having decided to continue his journey by boat, Tristram doesn't see why he should also pay for the coach he isn't taking: "Bon Dieu! what, pay for the way I go! and for the way I do *not* go!" The Commissary points out that he *may* go by coach if he chooses. Seeing that he must finally pay, Tristram decides to get his money's worth; he plays the part of the persecuted foreigner. The Commissary patiently explains that if one decides to discontinue his journey by coach, he must give notice two stops before; since Tristram didn't do this, he must pay the fare for two more stops.

Tristram feels that he has had his money's worth in wisecrack repartee, so he is content to note down his witty remarks. He suddenly discovers that his sheaf of notes (his "remarks") is missing, he remembers that he left them in the pocket of his coach, and he runs back to the purchaser's house. There he discovers that his remarks have been used as curl-papers, twisted around the hair of a "*French* woman's noddle." She gives them up graciously, and he collects them in his hat, remarking that when they are published, "they will be worse twisted still."

Lippius' clock—one of his sight-seeing targets—"was all out of joints, and had not gone for some years." He doesn't mind: "It will give me the more time...to peruse the *Chinese* history." As he gets near the college of the Jesuits, where the books are kept, he decides that he doesn't want to see them after all; he is anxious only to see the Tomb of the Lovers, and he rushes there eagerly:

> Tender and faithful spirits! cried I, addressing myself to *Amandus* and *Amanda*—long—long have I tarried to drop this tear upon your tomb—I come—I come—
> When I came—there was no tomb to drop it upon.

"Let me get rid of my remark upon Avignon," Tristram says. He decides that it may be too much of a generalization to say that "*Avignon* is more subject to high winds than any town in all *France,*" merely because his hat was blown off the first night he was there.

Having arrived in the south of France, Tristram feels that he has successfully left Death behind. He changes his mode of travel and decides to "traverse the rich plains of Languedoc" on muleback. He observes that "there is nothing more pleasing to a traveller—or more terrible to travel-writers, than a large rich plain"; the latter have nothing to comment about: "They have then a large plain upon their hands, which they know not what to do with—and which is of little or no use to them but to carry them to some town."

After a bit of commerce—he buys some ripe figs, planning to get the basket with them, finds two dozen eggs under them which he doesn't intend to buy, and the seller has no other basket for her eggs—he says that he is "hastening to the story of my uncle *Toby*'s amours." His last adventure—*his* "PLAIN STORIES" rather than those of a travel-writer— is set among the gay country folk, and he joins their pleasant dancing. Flirting gallantly with "a sun-burnt daughter of Labour," Nannette, he is distracted by "that cursed slit" in her petticoat: "I would have given a crown to have it sew'd up—*Nannette* would not have given a sous—*Viva la joia!* was in her lips—*Viva la joia!* was in her eyes."

He cannot stay; he dances off to "go on straight forwards, without digression or parenthesis, in my uncle *Toby*'s amours."

Commentary

The travelogue continues with more fun at the expense of travelogues, travelers, and sight-seeing. Of the four things he wanted to see at Lyons, one was broken, one was in the next town, one ceased to interest him, and one wasn't anywhere at all.

The sentimentalist in Tristram looks forward to dropping a tear at the Tomb of the Lovers; the ironist in him draws out the suspense and finishes it off with "there was no tomb to drop it upon." We have seen these two forces at work before, as in the scene of Uncle Toby and the fly and in the death scene of Le Fever. Tristram is moved by his sentimental impulses, but always only up to a certain point; as soon as it gets excessive or artificial, he merrily (and often, subtly) smashes his delicate creation. He is often quite frank about his motives in depicting certain sentimental subjects, and this has been disappointing to many softhearted readers over the past two centuries. The kindness of giving a sweet macaroon to an ass that has probably never eaten anything so good in its life is the smaller part of his motives: he was curious about *how* an ass would eat it.

The lengthy interchange with the Commissary is a fine example of non-communication between a "foreigner" and a "native." Tristram presents the discussion with all its nuances, not merely to show how stubborn the French are or how unsociable their customs; he deliberately puts off the explanation behind the Commissary's insistence on payment in order to show the comedy of two people who don't understand each other's point of view.

Tristram's "remark upon Avignon" is a clever summary of how impressionistic the guidebooks often are and how things get exaggerated.

The final part of the book shows Tristram in his natural devil-may-care attitude toward death. There is no reason to think that it is false. When he reaches the sunny south, he feels very much alive and well; he responds to that feeling, enjoying his pleasant journey to the full. He observes several times in the novel (as he did at the beginning of Bk. 7 and will do again in Bk. 8) that he has never let the imminence of death blacken his outlook or make his writing somber and serious. Indeed, when we see him dancing and flirting with Nannette, we don't believe that it can be true — it is — that he is dying.

The sensualist and the novelist seem to be fighting each other; *maybe* Tristram is serious when he says "Why could I not live and end my days thus?... dance, and sing,... and go to heaven with this nut brown maid?" It is hard to say whether the idyllic life is truly what he wants or whether it is merely another pretty picture that captures the imagination of the eighteenth-century intellectual. At any rate, his promise of Uncle Toby's amours drives him on, and in Bks. 8 and 9 we will get the whole story.

BOOK 8

Chapters 1-17

Summary

In spite of his clearly stated intention to go on to the story of Uncle Toby's amours, Tristram seriously doubts that he will be able to avoid "bastardly" digressions. He will, however, try his best.

Beginning with the half-sentence "It is with LOVE as with CUCKOLDOM — ," Tristram interrupts to talk about his way of beginning a book. He is confident that his way of doing it is the best (further, "it is the most religious"): "I begin with writing the first sentence — and trusting to Almighty God for the second."

After a little digression on his "great aunt *Dinah*'s old black velvet mask" — because the Shandy women have shown their faces in public, they have attracted fewer distinguished husbands — Tristram finishes his sentence, "It is with LOVE as with CUCKOLDOM — ": "the suffering party is...the last in the house who knows any thing about the matter."

Hearing about if finally from the servants, Uncle Toby had "to look into the affair."

Water-drinkers supposedly have "some tender nymph breaking her heart in secret for them," as a rule. Tristram doesn't really understand why "a rill of cold water dribbling through my inward parts, should light up a torch in my *Jenny*'s —," but it does. Unfortunately, Uncle Toby is not a water-drinker: "He drank it neither pure nor mix'd, or any how, or any where" if he could avoid it. Tristram's theory doesn't seem to work, and he himself is at a loss to explain what he is doing in this chapter: "One would think I took a pleasure in running into difficulties of this kind, merely to make fresh experiments of getting out of 'em." He enumerates his other troubles, among them this: "...and is it but two months ago, that in a fit of laughter, on seeing a cardinal make water like a...[choir boy] (with both hands)," he broke a vessel in his lungs and lost two quarts of blood. The doctors told him that if he had lost as much more, "it would have amounted to a gallon."

"But for heaven's sake,...let us take the story straight before us," Tristram says, as if we somehow have been leading him away from it.

When Toby and Trim rushed down to the country to start on their fortifications (Bk. 2, Chap. 5, and more recently, Bk. 6, Chap. 21), Shandy Hall was "at that time unfurnished; and the little inn where poor *Le Fever* died, not yet built." He didn't have a bed to sleep in, so "he was constrained to accept of a bed at Mrs. *Wadman*'s, for a night or two" until Trim could build him one in his own house. Seeing Uncle Toby in her house among her "goods and chattels," Mrs. Wadman begins to consider him a part of it; Uncle Toby "gets foisted into her inventory."

Mrs. Wadman has cold feet in bed, especially in the "many bleak and decemberly nights of a seven years widowhood." She wears extra-long nightgowns which her maid, Bridget, pins up at the bottom to keep her feet warm. The first night of Toby's stay she sat up until midnight, thinking; the second night she "took out her marriage-settlement, and read it over with great devotion"; the third night, "(which was the last of my uncle *Toby*'s stay)," as Bridget was about to pin up the nightgown, she "kick'd the pin out of her fingers." "From all which it was plain that the widow *Wadman* was in love with my uncle *Toby*."

Uncle Toby was busy, however, with the wars, and it wasn't until the demolition of Dunkirk (following the Treaty of Utrecht) — almost eleven years later — that he stopped being busy.

Tristram sympathizes with Widow Wadman because he says that he is like her in not being able "to go on and love...or let it alone," that is, make a decision one way or the other in the face of indifference. He loves and hates alternately the women who don't reciprocate his feeling, and he alphabetically summarizes the extravagant qualities of love.

The position of Widow Wadman's house enabled her to watch the campaigns on the bowling green: "She could observe my uncle *Toby's* motions, and was mistress likewise of his councils of war" because Bridget persuaded Trim to suggest to Uncle Toby that they put in a little gate between her yard and his. "...It enabled her to carry on her approaches to the very door of the sentry-box."

"It is a great pity," says Tristram, that a man "may be set on fire like a candle, at either end — provided there is a sufficient wick standing out." He prefers to be set on fire from the top, from his head to his heart to his liver and so on down. Widow Wadman "predetermined to light my uncle *Toby* neither at this end or that; but like a prodigal's candle, to light him, if possible, at both ends at once." The means were ready at hand: whenever a campaign was going on, Uncle Toby would tack up inside the sentry box "a plan of the place, fasten'd up with two or three pins at the top, but loose at the bottom...." And when the attack was ready, "Mrs. *Wadman* had nothing more to do, when she had got advanced to the door of the sentry-box, but to extend her right hand; and edging in her left foot at the same movement, to take hold of the map or plan,...and with out-stretched neck meeting it half way, — to advance it towards her." With his pipe, Uncle Toby would begin the explanation of the campaign. She would take the pipe from him under the pretext of "pointing more distinctly at some redoubt or breast-work in the map," but what she really wanted was to make him point with his finger. His hand seemed never to be pointing at the right place, Tristram says: "Mrs. *Wadman* had it ever to take up, or, with the gentlest pushings, protrusions, or equivocal compressions, that a hand to be removed is capable of receiving — to get it press'd a hair breadth of one side out of her way." And meanwhile, "her leg...slightly press'd against the calf of his." Among a "bundle of original papers and drawings which my father took care to roll up by themselves," Tristram has found a campaign map, and from the pin punctures and "snuffy finger and thumb" prints (which he takes to be those of Widow Wadman), he considers this theory to be confirmed.

Commentary

If anyone knows himself well, it is Tristram. The digressions that he "fears" will come between him and the straight-line story of Toby's amours amount to about 10 in the first 17 chapters! Couldn't they have been avoided somehow? Well, yes. There was an explanation early in the novel (among others) which it would be well to recall: "...If he is a man of the least spirit, he will have fifty deviations from a straight line to make with this or that party as he goes along.... He will have views and prospects to himself perpetually solliciting his eye, which he can no more help standing still to look at than he can fly" (Bk. 1, Chap. 14).

Tristram's guise of "careless disport" is on him again. He writes, he says, by putting down the first sentence, and God only knows what the second one will be. This nonchalance is so very convincing that it is almost a pity that it isn't true; the writer is almost unbelievably careful about the working out of the details, the interrelationship between the events and the ideas they stimulate both in himself and in the reader. He pretends that he doesn't know how but somehow it works: "...observe how one sentence of mine follows another, and how the plan follows the whole."

The digression on Aunt Dinah's mask and the effect of masks or their absence on the Shandy lineage is one of the many points at which the reader may be baffled. One often feels that the only way to solve the crux completely is by immersing oneself in eighteenth-century culture. There are many such reefs beneath the waters of *Tristram Shandy*.

Concerning Tristram's "difficulties" with his subject in Chaps. 5 and 6, one is safe in saying that it is true, that Tristram *does* take pleasure in running into difficulties so that he can try new ways of getting out of them. An important purpose is served by his reminding the reader that authors have problems: he is an author and he wants us to see him constantly and not get too wrapped up in "Shandy adventures." Another thing is that the culmination of the "amours" has to be put off as long as possible; therefore, when he gets to them in Chap. 10, he is going to begin again at the beginning for the nth time.

Still seriously ill, Tristram is able to tie his recent hemorrhage to the ridiculous sight of the cardinal making water. And the levity with which he treats doctors is consistent with the rest of his personality: the considered diagnosis of the doctors' was that four quarts make a gallon, i.e., two plus two equals four.

Widow Wadman is a pleasant creation. She wants a husband to help keep her feet warm in bed and to provide her with certain other creature comforts (as we will see in the next book). The wiles she uses to make Uncle Toby conscious of her love for him are as carefully planned as his own campaigns; the battles of the War of the Spanish Succession are paralleled by the battle of the sexes that she wages fruitlessly for the same 11 or 12 years (1701-1713). Humanity and its outlines are delicately drawn by the author: when she kicks the tucking-in pin from Bridget's hands, she is announcing her motives, her hopes, and her love in the single rakish movement. The movements of Eve, the seductress, have rarely been so beautifully described as they are by Tristram; the scene at the sentry box—she attacking in her own battle under the pretext of wanting to know about Uncle Toby's battle, he barely conscious of what is happening—is surely one of the subtlest descriptions of amatory maneuvers in literature. Tristram is more eloquent with fingers than some writers are with whole bodies; the abetting pressure of leg against leg is sexier, but unnecessary.

Supporting documents are again brought in to rationalize the author's omniscience (one of Toby's maps among Walter's papers), and Tristram the sentimentalist treasures the map for the past that it evokes.

Chapters 18-25

Summary

Trim informs Toby that "the fortifications are quite destroyed." Toby, "with a sigh half suppress'd," would like to confirm the details in the official "stipulation"; since he has put the action off for six weeks, the old charwoman finally burned the newspaper containing the stipulation. Trim is about to carry off his tools, but Toby's sighs stop him; he therefore plans to do it "before his honour rises to-morrow morning," to save him the pain of seeing it all come to an end.

To cheer up his master, Trim begins to tell him a story: The King of Bohemia and His Seven Castles. Before he can get started, however, Toby compliments and praises Trim for his good nature and character. Trim removes his hat and bows—although he is sitting down—and in so doing, he loses his grip on his hat. The hat lies on the ground just out of reach.

Trim begins his story: "There was a certain king of Bo - - he—" Toby interrupts to invite him to put on his hat again. They discuss the tarnish on the embroidery, and Trim is moved at the thought of his brother Tom, who had sent it to him from Portugal. Trim begins again: "There was a certain king of *Bohemia,* but in whose reign, except his own, I am not able to inform your honour — " "I do not desire it of thee, *Trim*, by any means, cried my uncle *Toby*." The next stop is caused by the date: "In the year of our Lord one thousand seven hundred and twelve, there was, an' please your honour — " " — To tell thee truly, *Trim*, quoth my uncle *Toby*, any other date would have pleased me much better...." Trim's nerves begin to get slightly raw; when Toby recommends that he use a different date "if ever thou tellest it again — ," Trim replies: " — If I live, an' please your honour, but once to get through it, I will never tell it again...either to man, woman, or child." Military matters arise in the discussion of the difference *geography* and *chronology;* from there they proceed to the justification for Bohemia's not having a seaport ("being totally inland") and then to predestination. Trim mentions that he was once in love, his destiny having arranged for him to be wounded in the knee first. They argue inconclusively about whether a wound is more painful in the knee or in the groin, and Mrs. Wadman, sitting in her garden on the other side of the hedge, "instantly stopp'd her breath — unpinn'd her mob at the chin, and stood up upon one leg."

Trim tells about the incident: he was being transported by cart with other wounded men; arriving at a peasant's house, he felt that he could not go farther. A kind young woman persuades them to leave Trim at the house, with the consent of the owner, and she undertakes to nurse him and see to all his needs. "By thy description, *Trim*, said my uncle *Toby*, I dare say she was a young *Beguine*" — one of those nuns who "visit and take care of the sick by profession — I had rather, for my own part, they did it out of good-nature." She took care of Trim for several weeks, and he grew very fond of her: "...my heart sickened, and I lost colour when she left the room," and yet, for a reason given in asterisks (and overheard by Mrs. Wadman), Trim is sure that *"it was not love."*

One Sunday afternoon, however, when the old peasant and his wife went out for a walk, Trim did fall in love. His wound was doing well, but "it was succeeded with an itching both above and below my knee." The "fair *Beguine*" said, "It wants rubbing a little," and she rubbed and rubbed. "I perceived, then, I was beginning to be in love," says Trim, and after a while, "my passion rose to the highest pitch — I seiz'd her hand — " " — And then, thou clapped'st it to thy lips, *Trim*, said my uncle *Toby* — and madest a speech." Tristram points out that "whether the corporal's amour terminated precisely in the way my uncle *Toby* described it, is not material."

Mrs. Wadman appears at that moment: "...the disposition which *Trim* had made in my uncle *Toby*'s mind, was too favourable a crisis to be let slipp'd." "I am half distracted, captain *Shandy*, said Mrs. *Wadman*, holding up her cambrick handkerchief to her left eye, as she approach'd the door of my uncle *Toby*'s sentry-box — a mote — or sand — or something — I know not what, has got into this eye of mine — do look into it." She "edged herself close in beside" him, and "squeezing herself down upon the corner of his bench," she says again, "Do look into it." He looks, but her "left eye shines this moment as lucid as her right...." Tristram sends a warning into the past: "There is nothing, my dear paternal uncle! but one lambent delicious fire, furtively shooting out from every part of it, in all directions, into thine— —If thou lookest, uncle *Toby*, in search of this mote one moment longer—thou art undone."

The eye is a beautiful one, and Tristram compares it with other eyes. Among other things, this eye says, " 'How can you live comfortless, captain *Shandy*, and alone, without a bosom to lean your head on — or trust your cares to?' " Tristram fears that if he continues, he will fall in love with it himself. At any rate, this eye "did my uncle *Toby*'s business."

Commentary

In Bk. 6, Chap. 34, Toby and Trim are about to destroy Dunkirk and finish off their fortifications. After that is done, Tristram will arrange for Toby to fall in love. But between that point and this, Tristram has inserted the story of his travels in France, the early years of the war games, and the growing but frustrated passion of the Widow Wadman for Toby. Now, at long last, the fortifications are leveled, and the real love scene can begin.

The story of the King of Bohemia and His Seven Castles, which ultimately provides the occasion for Mrs. Wadman to hypnotize Uncle Toby, is a very funny story—that is, the story *about* the story, since we never learn the end of the story itself. In these scenes between Trim and Uncle Toby we have another outstanding characteristic of the Shandy Heritage: nothing ever gets finished. Tristram obviously inherits part of his nature from Uncle Toby as well as from his father. Toby is part of the Shandy complex, as we see from the way he manages to interrupt, digress from, and generally interfere with the progress of the tale. Later, he recalls the event: *"Bohemia!* said my uncle *Toby* - - - - musing a long time - - - What became of that story, *Trim?"* " — We lost it, an' please your honour, somehow betwixt us." Tristram never finishes the story for us (possibly because he doesn't know the ending).

The tale of the "fair Beguine" shows us Trim in "love"; it also shows us the undeviating ingenuousness of Uncle Toby, who puts his own ending to Trim's story, a very romantic and highly improbable conclusion to what Trim was saying. Both Tristram and the eavesdropping Mrs. Wadman suspect that that wasn't what Trim was going to say.

Mrs. Wadman, that combination of Eve and the Serpent, appears with her troubled and troubling eye. The exposé of woman's wiles is again as subtle and as captivating as the previous scene in the sentry box, when fingers were the agents of flirtation (Chap. 16). The eloquence of Mrs. Wadman's eye — translated into English for us by Tristram — is irresistible; even Uncle Toby knows that that was when he was first smitten: " 'Twas just whilst thou went'st off with the wheel-barrow," he tells Trim later (Chap. 28).

Chapters 26-35

Summary

The author compares the different behavior in love of his father and his uncle. Toby was the opposite of Walter: he "took it like a lamb — sat still and let the poison work in his veins without resistance." Actually, he mistook it at first; riding his horse on an errand, he got a blister on his bottom, and when the pain remained after the blister had broken, he was convinced "that his wound was not a skin-deep-wound — but that it had gone to his heart."

He announces to Trim, "I am in love, corporal!" and considers the ways of letting the object of his passion know about it. "...As we are neighbours, *Trim*, — the best way I think is to let her know it civilly first." As they discuss various maneuvers, Mrs. Wadman and Bridget are holding a council on the same subject. There is something that worries the widow: "I am terribly afraid,...in case I should marry him, *Bridget* — that the poor captain will not enjoy *his health* [italics added], with the monstrous wound upon his groin." Bridget reassures her that the wound is healed, and since she assumes that Corporal Trim will be courting her while his master is courting her mistress, she promises to find out all from him. "I could like to know — merely for his sake, said Mrs. *Wadman*."

Toby and Trim discuss the proper uniform, Trim advising against the "red plush ones" because "they will be too clumsy." When Toby instructs Trim to polish up his sword, Trim dissuades him from wearing it: " 'Twill be only in your honour's way." Careful plans are made: "We'll march up boldly,...and whilst your honour engages Mrs. *Wadman* in the parlour, to the right— I'll attack Mrs. *Bridget* in the kitchen, to the left." Toby agrees with the plan, "but I declare, corporal I had rather march up to the very edge of a trench—."

Walter Shandy referred often to St. Hilarion's metaphor of *ass* for "body": self-punishment was "the means he [Hilarion] used, to make his *ass* (meaning his body) leave off kicking." Walter asks Toby, "upon his first seeing him after he fell in love—and how goes it with your ASSE?" Uncle Toby, "thinking more of the *part* where he had had the blister, than of *Hilarion's* metaphor," answers, "My A−e...is much better." General laughter "drove my father's Asse off the field." Mrs. Shandy asks Toby whether he is really in love, and he answers that it is true; "...and when did you know it? quoth my mother— " "— When the blister broke; replied my uncle *Toby.*"

Walter thinks that it is important for Toby to know which kind of love he is the victim of, "the Brain or Liver." The idea of Toby's marrying and having children worries him somewhat because he would cease to be Toby's heir. He recovers himself and goes on to talk of the goodness of Toby's potential offspring and the "system of Love and marriage" that Toby should follow; his guides should be Plato, Ficinus, and Valesius.

Apropos of his father's argumentativeness about the benefits of marriage, Tristram observes that "if there were twenty people in company— in less than half an hour he was sure to have every one of 'em against him." He doubts that there will be a wedding within a year in spite of the mutual "love" between Toby and Mrs. Wadman. Trim reassures Uncle Toby that Mrs. Wadman will fall in ten days. The company break up when Trim answers Dr. Slop's challenge of "whence...hast thou all this knowledge of woman, friend?": "By falling in love with a popish clergy-woman."

Before retiring for the night, Walter writes his brother a letter of advice about "the nature of women, and of love-making to them." It is full of hints on etiquette, on social discourse with women, and on the proper diet for lovers: "...and carefully abstain−that is, as much as thou canst, from peacocks, cranes, coots," etc.

Meanwhile, Toby and Trim plan their advance for 11 o'clock the following morning. Mr. and Mrs. Shandy are on hand to wish him luck and observe the skirmish. "I could like, said my mother, to look through the key-hole out of *curiosity* — Call it by it's right name, my dear, quoth my father — *And look through the key-hole as long as you will.*"

Commentary

Since Uncle Toby is as gentle as a lamb and like a lamb in many ways, Tristram compares him with the lamb going to the slaughter. The blister on his bottom is the catalyst in his awareness of being in love. Never having been in love before, he assumes that the pain — now unrelated to any obvious physical stimulus (since the blister has broken) — must be the pangs of love.

In this chapter (26) we find another of the "twice-removed" footnotes: Walter and Toby were riding out "to save if possible a beautiful wood, which the dean and chapter were hewing down to give to the poor.*...." At the bottom of the page there is this note: "*Mr. *Shandy* must mean the poor *in spirit;* inasmuch as they divided the money amongst themselves." Here, as in Bk. 2, Chap. 19, Laurence Sterne deliberately takes the role of editor, rather than that of novelist, in order to reinforce the fact that his book is about Tristram Shandy, the one who is doing all the writing and who sometimes makes mistakes.

Simple as a lamb, Toby thinks that he ought to go up to Mrs. Wadman and announce to her "civilly" that he loves her, but Trim talks him out of it. The maneuvers have to be gone through, in keeping with their absolutely military way of life: the element of surprise is most important in conducting an attack. The victim of the attack, meanwhile, is concerned about her future husband's sexual ability, a not unimportant matter to her. We will see how the entire theme of Toby's "amours" pivots on this question, and when it is finally resolved, we will wonder what we actually know about it.

There is a familiar pun in the mistaken metaphor. Toby doesn't deal in any metaphors other than military ones, and the point of Walter's reference to Hilarion's metaphor of the Ass is lost on him: to him, *ass* and *Arse* are the same thing, especially since there is an appropriate blister involved.

Walter's idea of improving the quality of mankind — if he were "an *Asiatick* monarch" — by putting Toby to stud with "the most beautiful women in my empire" is a generous one, although it doesn't meet with Toby's approval. It is typical of Walter's efficient procedures, and when he adds, "I would oblige thee, *nolens, volens* [willing or unwilling], to beget for me one subject every *month*," part of his statement catches the attention of his wife: "As my father pronounced the last word of the sentence — my mother took a pinch of snuff." It is clear that Mrs. Shandy is less than content with their monthly domestic "arrangements."

Erudition is especially useful in the sphere of love, in Walter's not so humble estimation. His letter to Toby contains all the impractical advice anyone could ever give. We can almost see Toby scratching his head and passing the letter over to Trim for explanation.

Mr. and Mrs. Shandy's stroll serves as the bridge between this book and the next installment. The chapter ends on a note of prurience: is Mrs. Shandy simply curious, or does she enjoy the role of peeping-Tom? The question will occupy some pages in Bk. 9.

BOOK 9

Chapters 1-15

Summary

Walter accuses his wife of prurience, then wonders whether he is perhaps being unjust to her. Strolling along, he glances into her eye and sees "a thousand reasons to wipe out the reproach." Her eye was a "blue, chill, pellucid chrystal with all its humours so at rest, the least mote or speck of desire might have been seen at the bottom of it, had it existed — it did not." Tristram wonders how he came by his lewdness, which he feels "particularly a little before the vernal and autumnal equinoxes."

Corporal Trim hasn't been able to do much with Uncle Toby's old wig and uniform; they remain quite shabby and worn. Still, Toby's nature is so obviously that of a gentleman, that "even his tarnish'd gold-laced hat and huge cockade of flimsy taffeta became him; and though not worth a button in themselves, yet the moment my uncle *Toby* put them on, they became serious objects...." He must wear the red plush breeches after all, since the thinner ones couldn't be turned again by the tailor.

On their way to the offensive, "my uncle *Toby* turn'd his head more than once behind him, to see how he was supported by the Corporal."

Trim waves his stick in encouragement, as if to "bid his honour 'never fear.'" But, says Tristram, "my uncle *Toby* did fear." He halts "within twenty paces of Mrs. *Wadman*'s door" and says "—she cannot, Corporal, take it amiss." Trim assures him that "she will take it, an' please your honour...just as the *Jew*'s widow at *Lisbon* took it of my brother *Tom*." Toby doesn't know the story, and Trim points out merely that Tom ended up in the clutches of the Inquisition: "'Tis a cursed place...when once a poor creature is in, he is in, an' please your honour, for ever." "'Tis very true; said my uncle Toby looking gravely at Mrs. *Wadman*'s house, as he spoke." When Trim adds, "Nothing...can be so sad as confinement for life—or so sweet...as liberty," Toby answers musingly, "Nothing, *Trim*."

Trim continues with the details of his brother Tom's adventure. Deciding to pay court to a sausage-maker's widow—left "in possession of a rousing trade"—Tom goes in to buy a pound of sausages and get acquainted. There he finds only a poor Negro girl, chasing away the flies, but "not killing them." Toby remarks, "'Tis a pretty picture!... she had suffered persecution, *Trim,* and had learnt mercy." After a brief interlude in which they discuss whether Negroes have souls ("I am not much versed, Corporal, quoth my uncle *Toby*, in things of that kind; but I suppose, God would not leave him without one, any more than thee or me"), Trim continues his story. Tom went into the back room to "talk to the *Jew*'s widow about love—and his pound of sausages," and he showed his usefulness by helping her with the sausage-making. "Now a widow, an' please your honour, always chuses a second husband as unlike the first as she can: so the affair was more than half settled in her mind before *Tom* mentioned it." Nevertheless, at some point, "she made a feint...of defending herself, by snatching up a sausage:—*Tom* instantly laid hold of another—." And so they were married.

The conference continues—still twenty paces from Mrs. Wadman's front door—and the two soldiers praise each other's good qualities, among them their readiness to "face about and march" into battle. "In pronouncing this, my uncle *Toby* faced about, and march'd firmly as at the head of his company—and the faithful Corporal, shouldering his stick,...march'd close behind him down the avenue."

"—Now what can their two noddles be about? cried my father to my mother." (They are standing by, watching the campaign.) "I dare say, quoth my mother————— But stop, dear Sir—for what my mother dared to say upon the occasion—and what my father did say upon it" are matters for another chapter (but not the next one).

Tristram feels the rush of time: "...the days and hours of it, more precious, my dear *Jenny!* than the rubies about thy neck, are flying over our heads like light clouds of a windy day, never to return more...whilst thou are twisting that lock, — see! it grows grey; and every time I kiss thy hand to bid adieu, and every absence which follows it, are preludes to that eternal separation which we are shortly to make. — — Heaven have mercy upon us both!" When he finishes his statement, he says, "Now, for what the world thinks of that ejaculation — I would not give a groat."

The author tells how Mr. and Mrs. Shandy in their strolling see Toby and Trim "within ten paces of the door." They stop to watch, and they see the gestures and movements as Trim tells the story of his brother Tom. As they watch, Toby and Trim face about and march back. When Mrs. Shandy wonders "What can their two noddles be about?" Mrs. Shandy answers, "I dare say...they are making fortifications." "— Not on Mrs. *Wadman*'s premises! cried my father, stepping back," and he proceeds methodically to damn fortifications, item by item. Mrs. Shandy agrees methodically with him, although Tristram points out that she probably didn't know what they were. But that is a quality that Tristram admires in her, especially "never to refuse her assent and consent to any proposition my father laid before her, merely because she did not understand it...." Further, she "would go on using a hard word twenty years together— and replying to it too, if it was a verb, in all its moods and tenses, without giving herself any trouble to enquire about it."

They discuss the possibility of children in the forthcoming union of Mrs. Wadman and Uncle Toby, and the "persuasion" necessary to produce those children. From a "sighing cadence of personal pity" in Mrs. Shandy's voice, Mr. Shandy suddenly becomes aware of the fact that it is the first Sunday of the month. "The first Lord of the Treasury thinking of *ways and means,* could not have returned home, with a more embarrassed look."

The author says that it is necessary to insert "upon this page and the five following [i.e., until Chap. 15], a good quantity of heterogeneous matter...to keep up that just balance betwixt wisdom and folly," which is essential to a good book. So for the next four chapters (12-15) he talks about his writing techniques and his desire to educate the public: "for never do I hit upon any invention or device which tendeth to the furtherance of good writing, but I instantly make it public; willing that all mankind should write as well as myself." (He adds: "— Which they certainly will, when they think as little.")

He indicates that there is a direct relationship between whether what he writes is "clean and fit to be read" and his laundry bills: the dirt gets on his shirts when he sets himself to clean writing. In one month he "dirtied one and thirty shirts with clean writing," but the critics do not appreciate the fact.

Still trying to get to Chap. 15, he thinks of the uses to which he can put Chap. 14. He doesn't get anything special done, however. Then, Chap. 15 arrives, and he is ready to "return to my uncle *Toby*."

Commentary

The reiteration of Walter's mild accusation neatly ties this final installment of *Tristram Shandy* to the last chapter of the previous installment; although two years intervened between publication of the two, the reader does not usually notice the slightest gap or change of tone.

The description of Mr. and Mrs. Shandy's stroll, her "tap of remonstrance" at his accusation, her misstep, his confusion and doubt, his "reading" of her eye is further proof of the author's sensitivity to the minutiae of human communication. But perhaps the author doesn't know his mother as well as he thinks he does (or perhaps he is just being waggish). When he admits his "lewdness"—and there is little question about that—he discounts the possibility of having inherited any of it from his mother. Yet he gives us a basis for thinking otherwise: in Bk. 8, Chap. 35, Mrs. Shandy takes a pinch of snuff—enabling her to sniff audibly—when Walter speaks of a month as the ideal interval for Toby's enforced "begettings"; in Chap. 11 of this book there is the suggestion that Mrs. Shandy feels sorry for herself because she is not sufficiently persuasive. That she is guileless is perfectly true, but that she is insensible does not follow in the least. We must make up our own minds about the truth of Tristram's statement that "a temperate current of blood ran orderly through her veins in all months of the year, and in all critical moments both of the day and night alike."

The statement in the second chapter about how the shabby, tarnished, and valueless uniform becomes a serious object when Uncle Toby puts it on has relevance to the material that Tristram uses in his book; many of the ideas and events—"not worth a button in themselves"—take on importance and seriousness when they become part of the Life and Opinions, when they are made to interact with more overtly meaningful ideas and events.

The march to Widow Wadman's house and the halt outside is ridiculous, outrageous, and completely understandable. Toby is as nervous as an adolescent, and Trim is reluctant to have a mistress side by side with a master. Everyone — Mrs. Wadman, Bridget, Walter, and Mrs. Shandy — is forced to hold his breath while the story of Tom goes forward. First, the story of Tom and the Inquisition is made to serve as model for Toby's forthcoming involvement with Mrs. Wadman; when Trim says that the Inquisition is "a cursed place," Toby sees Mrs. Wadman's house as a prison and he agrees. Loss of liberty through the offices of the Inquisition or through marriage with Mrs. Wadman is still loss of liberty.

The story proper occupies still more time, but it has its relevance: Trim began the story to prove to Toby that Mrs. Wadman would accept him as readily as the sausage-maker's widow accepted Tom. The bawdiness of the story is also appropriate; like the sausage-maker's widow, Mrs. Wadman is very much interested in a second husband "as unlike the first" one as possible. The irony lies in the difference between the modesty of Uncle Toby and the shamelessness of Trim's brother Tom. The little sub-story of the poor Negro servant furnishes the occasion for Toby's expression of kindness and compassion for the persecuted, whether he sees them or just hears about them in a story. The fact that the girl shooed away the flies rather than killed them must have made a great impression on Uncle Toby: 15 years later, when Tristram will be ten years old (it is now 1713), Toby himself will spare the fly he caught — the "overgrown one which had buzz'd about his nose, and tormented him cruelly all dinner-time."

The story serves the further purpose of distracting Uncle Toby and furnishing him with a basis for turning about face and marching away (away from, not toward, danger), to the dismay of all the observers.

The point of view then shifts, and we observe Toby and Trim through the eyes of Mr. and Mrs. Shandy — but not for long. Interrupting his mother's answers to his father, Tristram digresses with a series of very poignant images about the speed with which life passes: the days fly by like clouds before the wind, his Jenny's hair turns gray as he watches, each good-bye is a rehearsal for death. Although the sentiments ring true, they are still somewhat embarrassing to Tristram; he anticipates an unsympathetic response from his readers, and he answers it with bravado. The strange thing is that there is nothing self-pitying in this statement, especially since it would have been understandable; to borrow a fact from biography, we know that Sterne was dying at this time. He actually died 14 months after the publication of Bk. 9, but the long series of lung hemorrhages over a period of years made it quite clear that he could die at any time.

That digression over with, Tristram takes us back to the point of view established for Mr. and Mrs. Shandy in Chap. 8. They have been watching from the beginning, and we now see the movements of Toby and Trim from the beginning, without sound effects. Walter cannot figure out what is going on from Trim's and Toby's gestures (*we* of course already know), and it is amusing to try to reconstruct the scenes we have been through already just from the description of their movements. Mrs. Shandy is justified in thinking that they are about to start a new set of fortifications even if Walter *hopes* that it is impossible.

Their discussion of the foolishness of fortifications is an echo of the Beds of Justice scene in Bk. 6, Chap. 18; again, Walter proposes and Mrs. Shandy amiably agrees. Tristram gives us a little more insight into his mother's character and mentality, using them as a yardstick for his critics: if everyone were as unquestioningly agreeable as Mrs. Shandy, it would be a jollier world — especially for authors.

A little trick of Mrs. Shandy's — deliberate or not — is her use of Walter's statements to serve her own ends; it was he who brought up the matter of using persuasion in bed. She said "Amen" to his "Lord have mercy upon them," he said "Amen" to her "Amen," and she merely said it one more time. A message is eloquently conveyed without her sacrificing a bit of modesty.

Chapters 12-15 are another reminder of the author's pose of having only so much control over his book, of his having to conform with a certain inevitability in the material. The paradox of his having to allow the story to go its own way (the author as interpreter of events) and his balancing "wisdom and folly" (the author as creator) stands out once again. When he gets to Chap. 15, he is somehow able or ready to resume the narrative of the Amours.

Chapters 16-26

Summary

After their enthusiastic march away from Mrs. Wadman's house, Toby and Trim "recollected their business lay the other way; so they faced about and marched up streight to Mrs. *Wadman*'s door." Trim lifts the knocker, holds it for a minute. Bridget is behind the door "with her finger and her thumb upon the latch." Mrs. Wadman is sitting "breathless behind the window-curtain of her bed-chamber, watching their approach." "*Trim!* said my uncle *Toby* — but as he articulated the word, the minute expired, and *Trim* let fall the rapper." Uncle Toby whistles "Lillabullero." The door opens instantly, and Tristram says, "Let us go into the house."

Chapter 18 and Chap. 19 are blank pages, Chap. 20 begins with a large sprinkling of asterisks, and then we hear Uncle Toby saying to Mrs. Wadman: " — You shall see the very place, Madam." Mrs. Wadman blushes and blushes, and "for the sake of the unlearned reader," Tristram translates her blushes:

> "*L — d! I cannot look at it —*
> *What would the world say if I look'd at it?*
> *I should drop down, if I look'd at it —*
> *I wish I could look at it —*
> *There can be no sin in looking at it.*
> *— I will look at it.*"

More asterisks follow, and Toby says to Trim, " — I believe it is in the garret." Trim goes off. Returning to the sofa, Uncle Toby tells Mrs. Wadman, "You shall lay your finger upon the place." "I will not touch it, however, quoth Mrs. *Wadman* to herself."

The author realizes that there is a "mist which hangs upon these three pages," and he will try to dispel it and clear up everything. He asks the reader to "give me all the help you can."

There are "fifty different ends...for which a woman takes a husband," Tristram says, illustrating his point by the "imagery" of Slawkenbergius: a string of asses laden with panniers containing different things. One has empty bottles, the second tripes, the third "trunk-hose and pantofles," and so on; a lady examines the whole string of beasts until she comes to the one that carries "it." She "looks at it — considers it — samples it — measures it — stretches it...." And what is *it*, "for the love of Christ!" asks the reader, but neither Slawkenbergius nor Tristram is willing to answer. "We live in a world beset on all sides with mysteries and riddles," Tristram adds soothingly.

Uncle Toby's "fitness for the marriage state" was perfect, according to Tristram, but the "Devil...had raised scruples in Mrs. *Wadman's*

brain" about the wound. With reference to the metaphor Tristram took
from Slawkenbergius, the Devil had turned "my uncle *Toby*'s Virtue...
into nothing but *empty bottles, tripes, trunk-hose,* and *pantofles.*" We
are reminded that Bridget had promised she would find out all the details of Uncle Toby's wound — and its consequences — for her mistress
(Bk. 8, Chap. 28).

Suddenly the author gets cold feet about his story; he wants to
drop it: "...for though I have all along been hastening towards this part
of it, with so much earnest desire, as well knowing it to be the choicest
morsel of what I had to offer to the world," now that he has gotten to it,
he feels that it is too difficult. Since an "Invocation can do no hurt,"
Tristram invokes the "Gentle Spirit of sweetest humour, who erst didst
sit upon the easy pen of my beloved CERVANTES." The result is that he
is led to remember his trip through France and Italy. He talks of the
virtue of being a generous traveler, of not resenting having to pay a
little more because one is a foreigner ("how should the poor peasant
get butter to his bread?"; further, one gets a "sisterly kiss" from the
"fair Hostess and her Damsels" when one pays "with both hands
open"). At one point, while traveling in his coach, he hears "the sweetest notes I ever heard," played on the pipe by "poor *Maria*...with her
little goat beside her." He jumps down from the coach and sees a beautiful, demented young girl; feeling "the full force of an honest heart-
ache," he impetuously sits down between her and her goat. "MARIA
look'd wistfully for some time at me, and then at her goat — and then
at me — and then at her goat again, and so on, alternately — " " — Well,
Maria, said I softly — What resemblance do you find?"

Tristram entreats the "candid reader to believe me, that it was from
the humblest conviction of what a *Beast* man is, — that I ask'd the
question," and not from mere levity. Still, his heart smote him and he
resolved never to "commit mirth with man, woman, or child," for the
rest of his life; "as for writing nonsense to them — I believe, there was
a reserve." He bids Maria adieu and profoundly moved by the melancholy of her piping, "with broken and irregular steps walk'd softly" to
his coach. His next sentence is the final one of the chapter: " — What
an excellent inn at *Moulins!*"

Tristram feels that his "honour has lain bleeding this half hour"
because of the two blank chapters (18 and 19). No one will understand
why he did it, "for how is it possible they should foresee the necessity
I was under of writing the 25th chapter of my book, before the 18th,
&c.?" Although he will be called many "unsavory appellations," he will

not "take it amiss — All I wish is, that it may be a lesson to the world, *'to let people tell their stories their own way.'*"

The Eighteenth Chapter: Bridget opens the door, and Mrs. Wadman just has time to place a Bible on the table and come forward to receive Uncle Toby. He kisses her cheek — the custom — "march'd up abreast with her to the sopha, and in three plain words...told her, *'he was in love.'*" She "naturally looked down,...in expectation every moment, that my uncle *Toby* would go on." He, however, "when he had told Mrs. *Wadman* once that he loved her, he let it alone, and left the matter to work after its own way." Finally, she takes the initiative, pointing out the cares and responsibilities of the married state; since Toby is "so much at his ease," so well off, she wonders "what reasons can incline you to the state — ." His answer is that "they are written...in the Common-Prayer Book." And "as for children," says Mrs. Wadman, what *compensation* is there for the "suffering and defenceless mother who brings them into life?" Uncle Toby knows of none, "unless it be the pleasure which it has pleased God — ," and Mrs. Wadman interrupts with "A fiddlestick!"

The Nineteenth Chapter: Uncle Toby blushes at her "fiddlestick," although he doesn't know why. He feels "that he had somehow or other got beyond his depth," so he simply makes a proposal of marriage and leaves it "to work with her after its own way."

"It work'd not at all in her" because "there was something working there before." Tristram fears that he has already given it away, "but there is fire still in the subject — allons."

Chapter 26 follows. Tristram thinks that since Mrs. Wadman's first husband suffered constantly from sciatica — that painful neuritis of the hip and thighs — it is perfectly "natural for Mrs. *Wadman*...to wish to know how far from the hip to the groin...." She had studied anatomy and medical books, had borrowed "**Graaf* upon the bones and muscles," and she had questioned Dr. Slop at great length (the footnote: "**This must be a mistake in Mr. *Shandy;* for *Graaf* wrote upon the... parts of generation," i.e., the sexual organs). "Dr. *Slop* was the worst man alive at definitions;...in short, there was no way to extract it, but from my uncle *Toby* himself."

After asking many questions about the wound, its painfulness, its precise nature ("' — Was he able to mount a horse?' ' — Was motion bad for it?'"), after winning his heart with her interest and her humanity ("had he been worth a thousand, he had lost every heart of them to Mrs. *Wadman*"), she asks him "a little categorically," "—And where-abouts, dear Sir,…did you receive this sad blow?—In asking this question, Mrs. *Wadman* gave a slight glance towards the waistband of my uncle *Toby*'s red plush breeches, expecting naturally, as the shortest reply to it, that my uncle *Toby* would lay his fore-finger upon the place —it fell out otherwise—…."

Uncle Toby sent for the map of Namur, measured off the distance, and "with such virgin modesty laid her finger upon the place," that she didn't dare explain the mistake.

Commentary

Perhaps the validity for the "wisdom/folly" chapters is the actual passage of time—the time it takes us to read them—during which Uncle Toby and Trim can carry on their march to the rear, away from Mrs. Wadman's. They are finally back to the door, however, at Chap. 16. There is a splendid moment of frozen life in the scene where Bridget and Mrs. Wadman wait breathlessly for the sound of the knocker, Trim holds it suspended for a full minute, Uncle Toby sees his bachelor life passing before his eyes (as it were).

Tristram takes us in and then blanks out the scene. The action goes on, but a curtain has been dropped over it; we do not know what happened between the end of Chap. 17 and the continued action in Chap. 20 until Tristram thinks that it is time we learned about it in Chap. 25.

In Chap. 20 we are in the middle of a conversation, spoken and unspoken: Uncle Toby is telling Mrs. Wadman that she shall not only see the "very place," but she shall even put her finger on "it." She, in silent monologue, desires mightily to do so, although her modesty is sorely troubled. We assume—as she does—that "it" is Toby's wound, although we begin to be aware of a mutual misunderstanding on the part of the two principals.

Tristram digresses for three chapters—"in order to clear up the mist"—on a subject of interest to women. There is one thing women are most interested in, no matter what other excellent qualities a man may possess; and if that thing is lacking, all is lacking. When Tristram reminds us that Bridget had promised to find out from Trim all about Toby's wound, we have a better than vague idea of what Chaps. 21-23 are about.

The "choicest morsel" of his story again worries Tristram: can he do justice to it? As the reader is about to tear his hair in frustration, Tristram puts it off just a little longer. After all, where you have something as good as that to impart to the world, where is the harm in making the reader wait a bit? The Invocation fills in details of Tristram's recent trip to France (and Italy), described in Bk. 7, and we see the consistent generosity of the author-traveler. The basis for his kindness is a combination of "sentimental" feelings, self-interest, and true understanding of the needs of his fellow men — certainly a reasonable enough human response. The scene with Maria, her goat, and Tristram offers the author another opportunity for semi-malicious dissection of the gentler emotions: he is goat-like and Pan-like in his feelings toward the girl and not the kind, disinterested traveler that sentimental readers would like him to be. In spite of his disclaimer — he asked the question "from the humblest conviction of what a *Beast* man is" — Tristram's nature is showing. And if we still are in doubt about how "moved" he was, his comment on the excellence of the inn at Moulins should take care of that.

We find an important similarity between the death-scene of Le Fever (Bk. 6, Chap. 10) and the scene with Maria: Le Fever's pulse stops, goes, stops, goes; Maria looks at Tristram, then at the goat, then at Tristram, then the goat. In each case, the author pushes sentiment over the border of ridiculousness, as if to say, These delicate feelings easily become mushy feelings; protect yourself from that danger.

The author asserts the inevitability of his strategy in leaving blank the two chapters: it was necessary for the success of his storytelling, and that's that. "Let people tell their stories their own way" is his credo, and there is no other way that Tristram could have told this story (he says).

Chapters 18 and 19 are then given: the nonchalant lamb in the den of the tigress. Mrs. Wadman probes delicately for Toby's deeper motives, and he cannot or will not understand what she's getting at. Tristram has already told us what women want (Chaps. 21-23), and now he tells us what Mrs. Wadman, as a representative of women, wants.

Mrs. Wadman had an unsatisfactory married life with her first husband, owing to the immobility of his hips. She has been trying for a long time to figure out whether Toby's wound was similarly "incapacitating": Dr. Slop — no help — has been questioned, and medical tomes have been consulted. Once more, in connection with her prurient curiosity, author Sterne manages to kill two birds with one stone: his footnote again emphasizes the distance between himself as editor and Tristram as author, and he tells us precisely what Mrs. Wadman was interested in — as if we didn't know.

She is finally forced to ask Toby himself for the "whereabouts" of the "sad blow," and here — AT LONG LAST — we have the ultimate punch line, the "choicest morsel" itself: she glances demurely at his breeches, expecting him to point somewhere around there; he sends for the *map* and points to a completely different, completely uninteresting "whereabouts." He actually places her finger on the very spot — on the map of Namur.

Although the choicest morsel is not quite what we have been led to expect, there is no question about the choiceness of the whole situation: Widow Wadman's clamoring curiosity, Uncle Toby's ineffable unawareness, her fluttering, palpitating ambivalence about what she thinks she is about to feel and see, his heightening her expectation. And then comes the crash. Without doubt, this is the greatest and funniest anticlaimax in literature, and it could not have been achieved if Tristram had not led up to it so gradually, protracted it so elaborately, rearranged it so misleadingly.

Chapters 27-33

Summary

Corporal Trim carries the map away to the kitchen, and he proceeds to demonstrate the matter to Bridget. Miss Bridget, aware of her obligation to learn the truth, tries by telling Trim that she knows *for a fact,* "from credible witnesses," that Uncle Toby's accident had ********* him completely. Trim swears that " 'tis a story...as false as hell."

He woos Bridget successfully, and then he asks "whose suspicion misled thee?" She breaks down and "she then open'd her heart and told him all."

The campaign goes on each afternoon, neither master nor servant communicating anything to the other. Toby "had nothing to communicate," Trim "had much to communicate." One evening, Toby was "counting over to himself upon his finger ends...all Mrs. *Wadman's* perfections one by one." Getting confused in his calculations, he orders Trim to write them down as he dictates them. Of all her "thousand virtues," the one "which wins me most...is the compassionate turn and singular humanity of her character." Even if he were her brother, "she could not make more constant or more tender enquiries after my sufferings — *though now no more*" (italics supplied). Trim, after a short cough, dutifully writes at the very top of the sheet "HUMANITY."

In order to point out the difference between the wellborn lady and the maidservant, Toby asks Trim how often Bridget inquires about the wound on his knee. Trim answers that she never asks about it. Toby's triumph leads Trim to explain that if Toby's *knee* had been involved, "Mrs. *Wadman* would have troubled her head as little about it as *Bridget*"; the reason is that " 'the knee is such a distance from the main body — whereas the groin, your honour knows, is upon the very *curtin* of the *place.*'" Uncle Toby gives a long whistle — "but in a note which could scarce be heard across the table." Trim "had advanced too far to retire — in three words he told the rest — ." Uncle Toby lays down his pipe very gently: " — Let us go to my brother *Shandy*'s, said he."

Gossip and rumor have been at work, Tristram says as Toby and Trim march across to the Shandy household, and everyone for five miles around knew of the "difficulties of my uncle *Toby*'s siege, and what were the secret articles which had delay'd the surrender." Walter has just that minute found out about it, and he is furious "at the trespass done his brother by it." He insists that "the devil was in women, and that the whole of the affair was lust," and further, that "every evil and disorder in the world...was owing one way or other to the same unruly appetite."

Uncle Toby enters the room, "with marks of infinite benevolence and forgiveness in his looks," and Walter begins afresh in his diatribe against lust. He doesn't understand why "a race of so great, so exalted and godlike a Being as man" should depend for its continuance on sexual passion, which "couples and equals wise men with fools...." Some say that "like hunger, or thirst, or sleep — 'tis an affair neither good or bad — or shameful or otherwise." Yet what is the reason that "no language, translation, or periphrasis whatever" can be used to describe "the parts thereof...and whatever serves thereto" to a "cleanly mind"?

On the other hand, in ironic contrast, "the act of killing and destroying a man...is glorious — and the weapons by which we do it are honourable — We march with them upon our shoulders...." Toby and

Yorick are about to interrupt when "*Obadiah* broke into the middle of the room with a complaint, which cried out for an immediate hearing."

As the squire, Walter was obliged to keep a bull "for the service of the Parish." Obadiah had taken his cow to the bull on the same day that he himself got married, "so one was a reckoning to the other." When Obadiah's wife gave birth, Obadiah expected a calf daily (pregnancy in humans and cows being of equal duration). Six weeks more went by, and "*Obadiah*'s suspicions (like a good man's) fell upon the Bull." He tells Walter that "most of the townsmen, an' please your worship,... believe that 'tis all the Bull's fault." Dr. Slop confirms the fact that a cow is never barren, but he thinks of the possibility that Obadiah's wife might have borne prematurely.

He asks whether the child has hair on his head, and when Obadiah says, "It is as hairy as I am...*Obadiah* had not been shaved for three weeks," Walter gives a great whistle of relief at the narrow escape of his bull's reputation.

L - - d! said my mother, what is all this story about?——

A COCK and a BULL, said *Yorick*—— And one of the best of its kind, I ever heard.

Commentary

What Mrs. Wadman failed to learn from Toby, Bridget gets from Trim. The seductress is seduced, and the bawdy maneuvers are suggestively described by partial sentences and lots of asterisks. Poor Bridget learns that the wound did not after all ******** Toby, but in the process she confesses to Trim that her mistress has been extremely worried about the possibility.

Bridget obviously communicates to Mrs. Wadman the good news, i.e., what she learned from Trim, and Toby's courtship progresses satisfactorily. Everything would have worked out except for the most improbable circumstance of Toby's falling victim to a tiny sin of pride: Mrs. Wadman's great solicitousness about his groin wound and Bridget's complete apathy about Trim's knee wound demonstrate the difference between a lady and a servant. Trim explains, and Toby's pride goeth. Trim is not a long-suffering person; neither will he suffer in silence. We may assume that if he did not cherish the state of bachelorhood in which he and his master have lived happily and militarily, he would have resisted the great temptation to disenchant him. But that would be a different story.

Does Toby mind very much? We don't really know that, although we do know that it was a shock. On the night of Tristram's birth we are told about it; in "real" time it will be told on November 5, 1718, five years after this particular evening in which Toby goes to Walter's house, but in the novel it has already been told us in Bk. 2, Chap. 7: "I know nothing at all about them [i.e., women], — replied my uncle *Toby;* and I think...that the shock I received the year after the demolition of *Dunkirk,* in my affair with widow *Wadman;* — which shock you know I should not have received, but from my total ignorance of the sex, — has given me just cause to say, That I neither know, nor do pretend to know, any thing about 'em, or their concerns either." From this we know two things: 1) the book ends about five years before Tristram is born and 2) Toby's affair with Widow Wadman came to a definite end.

Toby has done his duty in this business of love: he looked into the eye and was enchanted, his blister burst and he believed he was in love, he declared it honorably and offered his hand in marriage. Whatever his love was, it was different from Mrs. Wadman's; the realization of this difference scared him off forever. If we remember him in front of Mrs. Wadman's house, we won't cherish for too long the vision of his disappointment.

At the Shandy household, the usual turbulent rhetoric is underway. Fortuitously—but plausibly—Walter has just heard the rumor about Mrs. Wadman's doubts of his brother's potency, and the topic of his harangue is The Lustfulness of Women. In spite of the bombast of Walter's anti-sexual position, there is some kind of grandeur in his speech and in his logic: on the one hand, man is "exalted and godlike," and on the other hand, the sexual act which perpetuates him is something that the "cleanly mind" cannot in any way speak about. Although Toby and Yorick are about to refute him, the contrast that he makes has its own kind of validity: killing and warfare are not shameful, and the "cleanly mind" does not hesitate to speak of the weapons and tools of destruction.

The final interruption is one of the best jokes of the book as well as one of the hardest to understand. Obadiah got married and took his cow to be bred on the same day; his wife bore, but his cow didn't. Like a good defense attorney, Walter tries to refute the charge that his bull is sterile, and in the hairiness of Obadiah's child, he finds his answer. Obadiah made a mistake and took his wife to the bull. He means that, although he doesn't say so; therefore Mrs. Shandy is puzzled. She asks, "What is all this story [*which* story?] about?" It is a Cock and Bull story, Yorick reassures her.

This is actually the second time that Walter accuses Obadiah of such a mistake: in Bk. 5, Chap. 3, Obadiah disclaimed any responsibility for the favorite mare's producing a mule. "See here! you rascal, cried my father, pointing to the mule, what you have done! — It was not me, said *Obadiah.* — How do I know that? replied my father."

So the "choicest morsel" has been told, the grandeur and the littleness of man have been argued about, and the similarity between man and beast has been presented in a parable masquerading as a joke. There is nothing else to do except to ask, like Mrs. Shandy, What is this story all about? It is a Cock and Bull story, and a cock-and-bull story, and various other kinds of story — and it is one of the best of its kind ever heard.

REVIEW QUESTIONS AND ESSAY TOPICS

1. In what way is it possible to reconcile the statement that the book will "be kept a-going" for forty years (Bk. 1, Chap. 22) with the contention that *Tristram Shandy* is a completed novel?

2. Tristram says that digressions are "the life, the soul of reading" (Bk. 1, Chap. 22). He is referring both to the necessary background material he has to bring in to explain matters and to his own thoughts about the story. Would you argue for or against his statement?

3. How much control do you think the writer has over the mixture of digression — both kinds mentioned in No. 2 above — and the Shandy history? Does he guide his pen or does his pen guide him?

4. Certain segments of *Tristram Shandy* are superficially boring and apparently impossible to read with any pleasure: Bk. 1, Chap. 20 ("the learned doctors of the Sorbonne"); Bk. 3, Chap. 38 ("Writers on the Nose"); Bk. 5, Chaps. 33-40 ("On Radical Heat and Radical Moisture"); Bk. 6, Chap. 19 ("Breeches in the literature of antiquity); and so on. Is there sufficient justification for such passages in the book?

5. Discuss the bases for considering the "I" of the book to be Tristram Shandy rather than Laurence Sterne.

6. Discuss the relationship between little Tristram and Tristram, the writer of the book, in the light of this statement: "...so far as

Tristram Shandy is concerned, Sterne never got beyond the boy's birth, baptism, and breeching. There are no opinions to be recorded of a lad who existed merely as an embryo or as an infant in his nurse's arms" (W. L. Cross, "Laurence Sterne in the Twentieth Century").

7. If you were a reader like the Lady in Bk. 1, Chap. 20, who reads "straight forwards, more in quest of the adventures, than of the deep erudition and knowledge," how would you feel about *Tristram Shandy?* Measure your answer in relation to what Samuel Johnson said about the novelist Samuel Richardson: "Why, Sir, if you were to read Richardson for the story, your impatience would be so much fretted that you would hang yourself."

8. What are some of the qualities that the writer of the book has inherited from his Shandy forebears?

9. In what ways does Tristram's book remind us of Walter Shandy's ideas and theories?

10. What kind of argument can you assemble to show that the following judgment is unreasonable and basically meaningless: "But though a great reader, Sterne was not a great thinker. His mind was alert and facile, and he displayed at times an intuitive logic, but he lacked the power of deep and sustained thought.... He was not even, in the best sense of the word, a learned man: nine-tenths of the 'erudition' of *Shandy* he took second-hand from compilers.... Rather he had a scrap-book mind that collected diverting information regardless of its importance or its source." In formulating your rebuttal, take into account the question of *purpose* and *intent*.

11. In Bk. 2, Chap. 7, Toby mentions an "unfortunate experience" with the Widow Wadman; four installments and seven years later, that story is completed. What does this indicate about the writer's plan and his control of what he was doing?

12. How sentimental and gushy is the writer of this book? Is kindheartedness necessarily mawkishness? Consider not only what the author says but how he says it.

13. Consider the elaborate details of certain small scenes, such as Walter's reaching for his handkerchief (Bk. 3, Chaps. 2-5), the description of the knots Obadiah tied in the green bag (Bk. 3, Chaps.

7-10), the position of Walter's hand (Bk. 4, Chap. 2), the dropping of Trim's hat (Bk. 5, Chap. 7). In what way are such details important to the author's method?

14. Discuss the pros and cons of the validity of Bk. 7 to the novel as a whole.

15. Are the bawdy passages and double entendres important in the book? Would you rather that they were deleted from it?

16. Discuss the character of Mrs. Shandy. Is she as stupid as she seems? Does she have redeeming qualities?

17. How successful is the author in the minor characters such as Susannah, Obadiah, Bridget, Dr. Slop?

18. Uncle Toby and Walter Shandy were, in the past, considered to be the main justification for the existence of *Tristram Shandy*. Comment on a version of the novel which presented only their stories with no digressions by Tristram.

19. If the story of Uncle Toby's amours is really a shaggy-dog story, does *Tristram Shandy* have sufficient other merits to allow it to "swim down the gutter of Time"? or should the reader say To heck with it?

20. Is it legitimate for an author to require—or even request—that the reader do things like "imagine to yourself...," draw a picture of Mrs. Wadman, replace misplaced chapters, and put up with omitted chapters?

21. Is the writer unable to present a straightforward story, or does he deliberately frustrate the reader? If the latter is true, what justification can there be for that?

22. Trace the digressive scheme of the first 20 chapters of Bk. 1 and discuss whether it has coherence and validity in relation to the "story."

23. Discuss the author's plan in the section between Bk. 1, Chap. 21, and Bk. 2, Chap. 6—the beginning of Uncle Toby's sentence "I think——" and the end of it. Take into consideration what the author says in Bk. 2, Chap. 8, about Duration, as well as his "loophole" at the end of that chapter.

24. Consider the view that the structure and form of *Tristram Shandy* tells us everything that we have to know about the author called Tristram Shandy, and that this character, Tristram, provides complete justification for everything unusual and unexpected in the book.

25. *Tristram Shandy* begins with a reference to sex and ends with another such reference. Is there any importance to this, or is it just the author's bawdiness?

SELECTED BIBLIOGRAPHY

Recommended Editions of *Tristram Shandy*

Tristram Shandy, ed. JAMES A. WORK. New York: Odyssey Press, 1940.

Tristram Shandy, ed. ALAN D. McKILLOP. New York: Harper & Brothers, 1962.

Tristram Shandy, ed. IAN WATT. Boston: Houghton Mifflin Co., 1965.

Essays, Books, and Articles

BAIRD, THEODORE. "The Time-Scheme in *Tristram Shandy* and a Source," *PMLA*, LI (1936), 803-20.

BOOTH, WAYNE C. "Did Sterne Complete *Tristram Shandy?*" *Modern Philology*, XLVIII (1951), 172-83.

CASH, ARTHUR H. "The Lockean Psychology of *Tristram Shandy*," *ELH*, XXII (1955), 125-35.

CROSS, WILBUR L. *The Life and Times of Laurence Sterne*, 2 vols. 3rd ed. New Haven: Yale University Press, 1929.

DILWORTH, ERNEST N. *The Unsentimental Journey of Laurence Sterne*. New York: King's Crown Press, 1948.

FLUCHÈRE, HENRI. *Laurence Sterne, de l'homme à l'oeuvre*. Paris: Gallimard, 1961.

FRYE, NORTHROP. "The Four Forms of Prose Fiction," *Hudson Review,* II (1950), 582-95.

HOLLAND, NORMAN N. "The Laughter of Laurence Sterne," *Hudson Review,* IX (1956), 422-30.

JEFFERSON, D. W. *Laurence Sterne* (Writers and Their Works, No. 52). London, New York, Toronto: published for the British Council and the National Book League by Longmans, Green & Co., 1954.

——. "*Tristram Shandy* and the Tradition of Learned Wit," *Essays in Criticism,* I (1951), 225-48.

LEHMAN, B. H. "Of Time, Personality, and the Author," in *Studies in the Comic.* University of California Studies in English, Vol. III, No. 2, 1941. Pp. 233-50.

MCKILLOP, ALAN D. "Laurence Sterne," in *The Early Masters of English Fiction.* Lawrence, Kansas: University of Kansas Press, 1956. Pp. 182-219.

MENDILOW, A. A. *Time and the Novel.* London: Peter Nevill, 1952. Pp. 158-99.

MUIR, EDWIN. "Laurence Sterne," in *Essays on Literature and Society.* London: The Hogarth Press, 1949. Pp. 49-56.

PARISH, CHARLES. "The Nature of Mr. Tristram Shandy, Author," *Boston University Studies in English,* V (Summer, 1961), 74-90.

READ, HERBERT. "Sterne," in *The Sense of Glory.* New York: Harcourt, Brace & Co., 1930. Pp. 123-51.

TOWERS, A. R. "Sterne's Cock and Bull Story," *ELH,* XXIV (1957), 12-29.

TRAUGOTT, JOHN. *Tristram Shandy's World.* Berkeley and Los Angeles: University of California Press, 1954.

VAN GHENT, DOROTHY. "On *Tristram Shandy,*" in *The English Novel: Form and Function.* New York: Rinehart & Co., 1953. Pp. 83-98.

WATKINS, W. B. C. "Yorick Revisited," in *Perilous Balance: The Tragic Genius of Swift, Johnson, and Sterne*. Princeton: Princeton University Press, 1939. Pp. 99-156.

Bibliography of Sterne

HARTLEY, LODWICK. *Laurence Sterne in the Twentieth Century: An Essay and a Bibliography of Sternean Studies, 1900-1965*. Chapel Hill: University of North Carolina Press, 1966.

NOTES

NOTES